THE ART OF PROBLEM SOLVING

THE ART OF

PROBLEM SOLVING

ACCOMPANIED BY ACKOFF'S FABLES

RUSSELL L. ACKOFF

Illustrations by
KAREN B. ACKOFF

JOHN WILEY & SONS
New York • Chichester • Brisbane • Toronto • Singapore

Library of Congress Cataloging in Publication Data:

Ackoff, Russell Lincoln, 1919-
  The art of problem solving.

  Bibliography: p.
  Includes index.
  1. Problem solving. I. Title.

HD30.29.A25   658.4'03   78-5627
ISBN 0-471-04289-7
ISBN 0-471-85808-0 (paper)

Printed in the United States of America

20 19 18

To
Daniel H. Silberberg
with
gratitude
and
affection

Between truth and lie are images and ideas
we imagine and think are real,
that paralyze our imagination and our thinking
in our efforts to conserve them.

We must continually learn to unlearn
much that we have learned, and learn to learn
that we have not been taught.
Only thus do we and our subject grow.

R. D. Laing, *The Politics*
of the Family and Other Essays
Vintage Books, New York, 1972

Preface

Over the years, I have been presented to audiences as an architect, philosopher, statistician, city planner, or operations researcher, or as a behavioral, communication, information, management, organizational, and systems scientist. But none of these tells me what I really am as well as did a characterization given to me by a student. He said I was a *problem solver*.

Problem solving is what I have been trying to do all my adult life, using whatever type of knowledge appeared accessible and relevant to me. In my "early period" I came to problem solving primarily from a *philosophical* point of view. In my "middle period" I came at it *scientifically*, keeping philosophy at my side. And now, in my "late period" I find myself preoccupied with the *art* of problem solving, keeping both philosophy and science ever at my side.

The more philosophy and science I tried to bring to bear on problem solving, the more I came to realize that even together they can assure us no more than adequate solutions to problems. They cannot provide exciting solutions, ones that we call "beautiful." Only the kind of problem solving that involves art can do this. And art implies creativity.

This is a book about creative problem solving. It is addressed to those who either make their living at, or derive their fun from solving problems—or both.

For me, the term "problem" does not refer to the kind of prefabricated exercises or puzzles with which educators continually confront students. It means *real* problems, the effective handling of which can make a significant difference to those who have them, even if they are philosophers and scientists.

This is neither a textbook, nor a handbook, nor a learned treatise. It it what is left from sifting through thirty years of experience, my own and others, in search of clues on how to make problem solving more creative and more fun. Solving even the most serious problems can be fun to the extent that we act creatively, and having fun in a creative way is also very likely to increase the quality of the solution it yields.

It will be apparent to even the casual reader that I had a lot of fun writing this book, much of it derived from the fact that my daughter Karen did its illustrations. Having her do them turned out to be the only way I have found to get her to read anything I have written.

I was assisted greatly in preparing the final version of this book by suggestions made by Paul A. Strassmann. Whenever I doubted whether writing this sort of thing was my "ball of wax," my good friend Stafford Beer encouraged me to keep at it. I hope he will not be sorry.

RUSSELL L. ACKOFF

Philadelphia, Pennsylvania
January 1978

Contents

THE ART OF PROBLEM SOLVING

PART ONE—the art

CHAPTER ONE

Creativity and Constraints

Most managers and management educators have a list of what they consider the essential properties of good management. I am no exception. My list, however, is unique because all the characteristics, properly enough, begin with C:

Competence
Communicativeness
Concern
Courage
Creativity

The greatest of these is creativity.

Without creativity a manager may do a good job, but he cannot do an outstanding one. At best he can preside over the progressive evolution of the organization he manages; he cannot lead it to a quantum jump—a radical leap forward. Such leaps are required if an organization is to "pull away from the pack" and "stay out in front." Those who lack creativity must either settle for doing well enough or wait for the breaks and hope they will be astute enough to recognize and take advantage of them. *The creative manager makes his own breaks.*

Educators generally attempt only to develop competence, communicativeness, and (sometimes) concern for others in their students. Most of them never try to develop courage or creativity. Their rationalization is that these are innate characteristics and hence can be neither taught nor learned.

Figure 1.1.

That creativity can be acquired seems to follow from the fact that it tends to get lost in the process of growing up. Adults recognize that young children, particularly preschoolers, are full of it. I recall a dramatic illustration of this point given by an eminent student of creativity, Edward de Bono, in a lecture to an audience consisting of managers and management scientists. He drew a picture on the blackboard of a wheelbarrow with an elliptical wheel (Figure 1.1) and asked the audience why it had been designed that way. There was a good deal of squirming, murmuring, and embarrassed tittering, but no answer. De Bono waited, letting the discomfort grow. He then told his audience that he had recently asked the same question of a group of children and almost immediately one of them had rushed to the board and drawn a squiggly line such as that shown in Figure 1.2. "The wheelbarrow is for a bumpy road," the child had said. The audience blushed and laughed self-consciously.

Most of us take for granted both the creativity of children and its subsequent loss. We do not try to understand, let alone prevent, this loss. Yet the disappearance of creativity is not a mystery; the explanation lies in a query that Jules Henry (1963), an American anthropologist, once made: What would happen, he asked,

> . . . if all through school the young were provoked to question the Ten Commandments, the sanctity of revealed religion, the foundations of patriotism, the profit motive, the two party system, monogomy, the laws of incest, and so on . . . . (p. 288)

The answer to Henry's question is clear: society, its institutions, and the organizations operating within it would be radically transformed by the inquisitive generation thus produced. Herein lies the rub: most of the affluent do not want to transform society or its parts. They would rather sacrifice what future social progress creative minds might bring about than run the risk of losing the products of previous progress that less creative minds are managing to preserve. The principal benefi-

Figure 1.2.

ciaries of contemporary society do not want to risk the loss of the benefits they now enjoy. Therefore, they, and the educational institutions they control, suppress creativity before children acquire the competence that, together with creativity, would enable them to bring about radical social transformations. Most adults fear that the current form and functioning of our society, its institutions, and the organizations within it could not survive the simultaneous onslaught of youthful creativity and competence. Student behavior in the 1960s convinced them of this.

The creativity of children is suppressed at home and at school where, Jules Henry (1963) remarked, "What we see is the pathetic surrender of babies" (p. 291). The eminent British psychiatrist Dr. Ronald Laing (1967) reinforced this observation: "What schools must do is induce children to want to think the way schools want them to think" (p. 71). Schools want them to think the way parents want them to think: conservatively, not creatively.

It is easy to see how schools suppress creativity in children. For example, when one of my daughters was in her early teens she came into my study one night with an extra-credit problem that her mathematics teacher had assigned for homework. On a sheet of paper distributed by the teacher were nine dots that formed a square (see Figure 1.3).

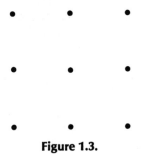

Figure 1.3.

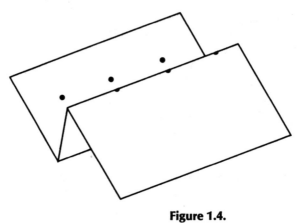

Figure 1.4.

The instructions below the figure said that a pen or pencil was to be placed on one of the dots and then four straight lines were to be drawn without lifting the pen or pencil from the paper so that all nine dots were covered by the lines.

My daughter had tried to solve the problem, with no success. She asked me for help, assuring me she would not claim the solution as her own. I recognized the problem, but I was unable to recall or find its solution. Impatient to get back to the work she had interrupted, I told her to forget about the problem. "It's not that important," I said. She left unconvinced and with an obviously lowered opinion of my problem-solving ability.

A short while later I heard her sobbing in the next room. I went in to see what was wrong. She told me she was ashamed to go to school without a solution to the problem. I invited her into my study and said that this time I would make a "real try." She came skeptically.

I knew, for reasons considered later, that a puzzle is a problem that we usually cannot solve because we make an incorrect assumption that precludes a solution. Therefore, I looked for such an assumption. The first one that occurred to me was that the paper had to remain flat on a surface while the lines were drawn. Once this assumption came to mind and I put it aside, a solution came quickly. I folded the sheet "in" across the middle line of dots and "out" across the bottom line so that the bottom dots fell on top of the dots of the top line (see Figure 1.4). Then, using a felt-tipped pen I drew a line through the top line of dots, holding the pen against the folded edge on which the bottom dots were located. Keeping my pen on the last dot, I unfolded the paper and flattened it. There was a line through the top and bottom rows of dots

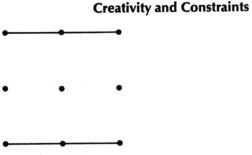

Figure 1.5.

(see Figure 1.5). With three lines left it was easy to cover the remaining dots (see Figure 1.6).

My daughter was delighted with the solution, and her faith in me was partially restored. I returned to my work with more than a little self-satisfaction.

When I returned from work the next day I could hardly wait to hear what had happened in my daughter's class. She returned my greeting as I entered with her usual "Hi" but nothing more. I waited a few moments and then asked, "Well, what happened in your math class?"

"It doesn't matter," she replied, not looking at me.

"Yes it does," I countered. "Now come on, tell me."

"It will only get you mad," she said.

"Maybe it will, but if it does, I will not be mad at you. So tell me."

"Well," she said, "the teacher asked the class who had solved the problem. About five of us raised our hands. She called on another girl who had her hand up and asked her to go to the board and show her solution. She did." My daughter then drew the solution shown in Figure 1.7 on a sheet of paper. It was the solution I had once known but forgotten.

"Then what happened?" I asked.

"The teacher congratulated the girl, told her to return to her seat,

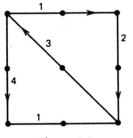

Figure 1.6.

Figure 1.7.

and started to talk about something else. I raised my hand. She stopped and asked me what I wanted. I told her I had a different solution to the problem, one you had given me. She was annoyed but asked me to go to the board and show it to the class. I told her I couldn't show it on the blackboard and needed to use the large pad on the easel in the corner of the room. She told me to go ahead. I drew the nine dots on a blank sheet and started to fold it when she asked what I was doing. I told her I was folding the paper. She told me I couldn't do that. I told her that the instructions didn't say I couldn't. Then she told me she didn't care what the instructions said; that was what she meant. She told me to sit down, so I never got to finish showing the solution."

This is how creativity is suppressed, although usually not so overtly. The teacher made it clear to her class that the objective of the assignment was not to find a solution to the problem, but to find *the* solution *she knew* and could pretend to have discovered on her own. She had no interest in any other solution.

Is it any wonder that students become more concerned with what a teacher expects of them in an examination than with what are the best answers to the questions asked?

Imagine what a teacher interested in promoting creativity could have done with the situation involving my daughter. She could have revealed the common property of both solutions: *they broke an assumption that the solver imposed on the problem.* In the teacher's solution the broken assumption was that the lines drawn had to lie within the perimeter of the square formed by the dots. She could then have gone on to encourage the students to find other solutions. Had she done so, one of the students might have discovered how to fold the paper so that *one* line drawn with a felt-tipped pen can cover all the dots (see Figure 1.8).

A puzzle is a problem that one cannot solve because of a *self-imposed constraint.* Creativity is shackled by self-imposed constraints. Therefore, the key to freeing it lies in developing an ability to identify such constraints and deliberately removing them.

It is not enough to become aware of the fact that self-imposed constraints are what obstruct creative problem solving. For example, now that you are aware of this fact, consider this problem.

If you have a balance scale, what is the minimum number of weights required to weigh objects of any number of pounds from one to forty?

Stop here and try to find the solution.

If you are like most people you reasoned somewhat as follows. It is

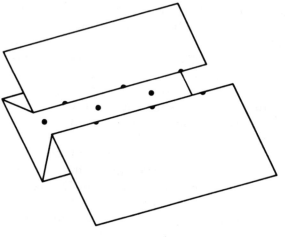

Figure 1.8.

obvious that a one-pound weight is needed to weigh a one-pound object. A two-pound weight is needed to weigh a two-pound object. A three-pound weight is not needed because the one- and two-pound weights can be added. A four-pound weight is needed but not a five $(4 + 1 = 5)$, six $(4 + 2 = 6)$, or seven $(4 + 2 + 1 = 7)$. An eight-pound weight is needed. This will get us up to fifteen pounds. A sixteen-pound weight is needed. This will get us up to thirty-one pounds. Finally, a thirty-two-pound weight is needed, and this will get us up to sixty-three pounds, more than the forty required. Therefore, the answer is six weights (1, 2, 4, 8, 16, and 32).

Wrong! The answer is four weights. Even after giving the right answer, most people cannot see what they missed. In the six-weight solution it was assumed that the object to be weighed must be placed on one side of the balance and the weights on the other, but this is a self-imposed constraint. Objects and weights can be placed on the same side of the scale. Once we "see" this, we find that only one-, three-, nine-, and twenty-seven-pound weights are necessary. For example, to weigh a two-pound object, we place the object and a one-pound weight on one side and the three-pound weight on the other. Similarly, if we put a seven-pound object and a three-pound weight on one side, we can put a nine- and a one-pound weight on the other.

Principles that guide our searches for self-imposed constraints are obviously helpful, but it has been my experience that they do not provide sufficient guidance to creative problem solving. It often takes a bigger push than a principle can provide to get over the hump of a self-imposed constraint. I have found that *examples,* real ones drawn from life, are often more effective because they are likely to be remembered better and longer. Therefore, I use them throughout the book.

The guides to creative problem solving that I suggest are based on an analysis of the nature of problems and an extended experience with management-oriented research projects. Therefore, it may be helpful to reveal the analysis of problem solving from which the suggestions I make are partially derived.

A problem, as I conceptualize it, has five types of component.

1. The one(s) faced with the problem, the *decision maker(s).*

The decision maker may be a group, large or small, or an individual.

2. Those aspects of the problem situation the decision maker can control: *the controllable variables.*

For example, in buying an automobile, the buyer can control such things as the make and model he buys, which accessories he adds, how he finances the purchase, and so on. These variables may be either quantitative (e.g., the number of doors) or qualitative (e.g., the color).

Choice or decision making consists of taking a course of action defined by values of one or more controlled variables. There must be at least two courses of action available, otherwise there is no choice and therefore no problem. There may, of course, be an unlimited number of courses of action available.

3. Those aspects of the problem situation the decision maker cannot control but those which, together with the controlled variables, can affect the outcome of his choice: the *uncontrolled variables.*

These may also be either quantitative or qualitative. Together they constitute the *problem environment.*

For example, the sales taxes on the purchase price of an automobile and the cost of licensing it are not controlled by the purchaser, but they affect the outcome, the cost of the purchase. Note that uncontrolled variables are not necessarily uncontrol*lable;* they may be controlled by others. Sales taxes are controllable by legislators. Some uncontrolled variables such as the weather are not subject to anyone's control. Orders for products received by a production department may be out of the control of the production manager, but under the control of the marketing manager. Furthermore, in a hierarchical organization each level controls something that lower levels cannot.

4. *Constraints* imposed from within or without on the possible values of the controlled and uncontrolled variables.

For example, the purchaser of an automobile may place a limit on how much he is willing to spend. He may also decide that he will not buy a used car. His choices may also be constrained by what is available at the time of purchase.

5. *The possible outcomes* produced jointly by the decision maker's choice and the uncontrolled variables.

For example, he may get either a good car or a "lemon." Note that there must be at least two possible outcomes. If this were not the case, the decision maker's choice would have no effect on the outcome; therefore, his choice would not be a "real" or "meaningful" one. Furthermore, the two or more possible outcomes must be *unequally* desirable; their values to him must be different, otherwise it would not matter to him which outcome occurred.

To one individual there may be no significant difference between the values of two automobiles of the same make and model but of different colors. To another this difference may be of great significance, in fact, critical.

A decision maker tries to select a course of action that produces an outcome he desires, one that is *efficient* relative to what he *values*. Such courses of action are said to be *effective*. Effectiveness is the product of efficiency and value. One who seeks the best, the most effective, course of action is said to *optimize*. One who seeks a solution that is good enough is said to *satisfice*.

In summary, choice exists only (1) when there are at least two possible courses of action available to the decision maker, (2) where there are at least two possible outcomes of unequal value to him, and (3) where the different courses of action have different effectiveness. In other words, choice exists when the action of the decision maker makes a difference in the value of the outcome.

Not every choice situation is a problem situation, but every problem involves a choice. A problem arises when the decision maker has some *doubt* about the relative effectiveness of the alternative courses of action. The solution process is directed at dispelling doubt.

It is apparent that a choice situation that presents a problem to one person may not do so to another because of a difference in their doubts. This is what makes for consultants, experts, advisors, and so on.

In dealing with a problematic situation, a decision maker must develop a *concept*—a representation or a model—of it. He attempts to solve the problem *as he conceives it*. Thus if his conception is wrong, the solution to the problem as conceived may not solve the problem as it exists. A common example is a formulation of a problem that leads to the suppression of symptoms rather than the removal of the cause of a deficiency that creates the problem. Because of such errors of conceptualization, it has often been observed that we more frequently fail to face the right problem than fail to solve the problem we face.

The conception of a problem that I have presented has a general form that can be represented by the equation:

The value of the outcome = A specified relationship
between
the controlled variables
and
the uncontrolled variables.

This equation may be subject to constraints on the controlled and uncontrolled variables.

A problem is said to be *solved* when the decision maker selects those values of the controlled variables which *maximize* the value of the outcome; that is, when he has optimized. If he selects values of the controlled variables that do not maximize the value of the outcome but produce an outcome that is good enough, he has *resolved* the problem by satisficing. There is a third possibility: he may *dissolve* the problem. This is accomplished by changing his values so that the choices available are no longer meaningful. For example, the problem of selecting a new car may be dissolved by deciding that the use of public transportation is better than driving oneself. It may also be dissolved by moving to within walking distance from work so that driving is no longer required. We use "solving" loosely to cover all three alternatives.

Now to the question, What is the meaning of "art" in "the art of problem solving"? Normally, "art" used in this way has nothing to do with aesthetics. For most people aesthetics has no relevance to problem solving. The "art of problem solving" usually refers to both our inability to understand problem solving completely and our ability to make decisions despite this deficiency. This is not the sense in which I use the concept; I use it in its aesthetic sense. To make sense of this I must go back in history.

14 The Art

The philosophers of ancient Greece divided the pursuits of man into four major categories:

1. The scientific—the pursuit of truth
2. The political-economic—the pursuit of power and plenty
3. The ethical-moral—the pursuit of goodness and virtue
4. The aesthetic—the pursuit of beauty

These categories were refined out of the philosophical thought of centuries; they were not the products of a deliberate effort to divide man's activities into exclusive and exhaustive categories. Obviously they are not exclusive, since two or more can be pursued simultaneously. Nevertheless, I believe these categories are exhaustive for reasons discussed later.

It is not surprising that we fail to reflect sufficiently on or fully understand the meaning of "aesthetics of problem solving." Over the last twenty-five centuries very few philosophers have been able to incorporate aesthetics into a comprehensive philosophical system, and there has been little systematic development of aesthetics. On the other hand, aestheticians tend to give the other three categories of man's activities short shrift. As a result, we understand aesthetics much less than science-technology, political economy, or ethics-morality. It is safe to say that most of us have some idea of the way each of these three aspects of our activity relates to the others, but no idea of how any of them relates to aesthetics.

Thoughtful persons would agree that considerable progress has been made in science and technology. Some, but perhaps fewer, would also agree that progress has been made in the domains of political economy and ethics-morality. However, one would be surprised to hear it argued that mankind has made aesthetic progress—that the products of our art are better than those of the ancients or even those of more recent eras.

It has become traditional for affluent people to separate work from play and hence from pleasure. They are conscious of aesthetics—or at least they know of the interaction of beauty, play, and pleasure—in their homes and their recreational and social activities. However, their attitudes toward business and work have been dominated by the Puritan ethic. This ethic contrasts work with play. It conceptualizes work as an *ascetic*, not an aesthetic, activity. Work—and problem solving is considered to be work—is widely thought of as both necessary and necessarily unpleasant. The dissatisfaction it has produced is rationalized by many apologists of the Industrial Revolution who argue that it should be accepted, if not embraced, as a kind of earthly purgatory in which sin is expiated and virtue is gradually accumulated.

It is hardly necessary to point out that, just as fun has been taken out of the work most adults do, it has also been taken out of the learning most children are forced to do. There is little that is beautiful in education.

A principal objective of my effort here is to put beauty and fun back into at least that aspect of work and education we call problem solving.

To understand the meaning of the aesthetics or art of problem solving, we must understand the effort made by philosophers throughout recorded history to find one desire that is both universal and ultimate in terms of which progress can be measured. This has been a search for an ideal shared by all men and women, past, present, and future. Searches for such an ideal failed, ironically, because those conducting the search were too sophisticated. Let me explain.

Once upon a time there was a young man who was granted three wishes. We all know that with the first two he managed to get himself into such a mess that he had to use his last wish to get back to his initial state. On hearing any one of the many versions of this story, most bright children tell us they could do better with only one wish: *they would wish that all their wishes would come true*. My teacher, the much-too-little recognized philosopher Edgar Arthur Singer, Jr. (1948) systematized this childlike wisdom by identifying a desire so universal that it unifies all men at all times. It is the desire for the ability to satisfy desires whatever they may be, even the desire for nothing, Nirvana. It is in the nature of purposeful systems—and people are purposeful systems—to desire, and one can desire nothing without desiring the ability to satisfy it. The ability to satisfy all desires is an ideal necessarily shared by all men at all times. It is called *omnipotence*. Its ideal character is reflected in the fact that virtually every religion ascribes it to deity.

Omnipotence is an ideal that, if it could be attained, would assure fulfillment of all other desires and therefore of all other ideals. Consequently, it is what might be called a *meta-ideal*.

There are four conditions that are necessary and sufficient for the continuous and simultaneous progress of *every* person toward omnipotence.

First, such progress requires a continual increase in the efficiency of the means by which we can pursue our ends and, therefore, a continual incease in our information, knowledge, and understanding—an increase in our grasp of truth. It is the function of science to provide such an increase, and the function of technology to provide an ability to use the products of science effectively.

Second, progress toward omnipotence requires a continuous increase in the availability of and access to those resources needed to employ the most efficient means available. Availability implies a state of plenty and access implies a state of power. To provide these is the function of the political economy.

Third, it requires continuous reduction of conflict within and between individuals, because conflict means that the satisfaction of one (or one's) desire precludes the satisfaction of another (or another's) desire. Therefore, we pursue both peace of mind and peace on earth, a state of goodness and virtue. This pursuit is ethical-moral.

Finally, it requires the aesthetic function. This is the most difficult to understand.

If man is to continually pursue the ideal of omnipotence, he must never be willing to settle for anything less; that is, he must never be either permanently discouraged or completely satisfied. Whenever he attains one objective, he must then start after another that is even more valuable to him, and he must seek a continual increase in his ability to satisfy his desires. Therefore, he must always be able to find new possibilities for improvement and satisfaction. He must always be able to generate visions of a more desirable state than the one he is in.

E. A. Singer, Jr. (1948) showed that it is the function of art to provide such visions and to *inspire* us to their pursuit: to create the creator of visions of the better and to give this creature the courage to pursue his visions no matter what short-run sacrifices are required. Inspiration and aspiration go hand in hand. *Beauty* is that property of the works and workings of man and Nature that stimulates new aspirations and commitments to their pursuit. No wonder we say of a solution to a problem that inspires us, "it is beautiful."

Long before Singer, Plato conceived of art as a stimulant that was potentially dangerous to society because it could threaten society's stability. His conception of the disquieting function of art is the same as that put forward here, but his conception of utopia, his *Republic,* as a stable state is not. There is at least as much satisfaction to be derived from the pursuit of objectives as in attaining them, and from the pursuit of solutions to problems as in attaining them. Therefore, in an ideal state, as I conceive it, man would not be problem free, but he would be capable of solving a continual flow of increasingly challenging problems.

Of greater importance is the fact that an ideal state is not attainable whatever its characteristics; therefore, in all less-than-ideal states such disquiet as Plato sought to control is required if continual progress toward the ideal is to be made.

In contrast to Plato, Aristotle viewed art as cathartic, a palliative for dissatisfaction, a producer of stability and contentment. Whereas Plato saw art as a producer of dissatisfaction with the present state of affairs that leads to efforts to create a different future, Aristotle saw it as a producer of satisfaction with what has already been accomplished. Plato saw art as *creative* and Aristotle saw it as *recreative*.

These are not different things but two aspects of the same thing. Art is both creative and recreative. These aspects of it can be viewed and discussed separately, but they cannot be separated. Recreation is the extraction of pleasure here and now, a reward for past efforts. It provides "the pause that refreshes" and by so doing *recreates the creator*. Art also produces an unwillingness to settle for what we have. It pulls us from the past and pushes us into the future.

Thus, to make problem solving creative (inspiring) and fun (recreative) is to put art into it. To do so is to reunite work, play, and learning and therefore to reunify man, at least in his problem-solving activities.

So much for my concept of the nature of problem solving and the art on which this guide is based.

Using the conception of a problem set forth above we can consider problem solving with respect to what the decision maker does about each of these components:

1. Objectives: desired outcomes
2. Controlled variables: courses of action
3. Uncontrolled variables: the environment
4. The relationships among these three

Since constraints apply to each of these, they need not be treated separately.

As stated previously, the principles presented are illustrated by a number of cases; I can vouch for most of them. A few are second hand or more, but the possible inaccuracies in my account of these cases in no way detracts from their usefulness as examples of the principles. As one of my friends said about these examples, "If they are not true, they ought to be." The reader may treat all the short illustrations as fictional. To assist him in doing so I present them in a form that one of my students named *Ackoff's Fables*. In these fables I use "Aesop," appropriately I hope, as a pseudonym for the creative problem solver.

Not all the fables have happy endings; they are not all success stories. Creative solutions are often not accepted. This is not surprising in view of the widespread resistance to change, particularly to something new and unconventional. Because of such resistance the creative problem solver is not likely to be successful unless he is also competent, communicative, concerned, and, most of all, courageous.

One final note: many of the cases used here have been used in previous writings but in different forms and for different purposes. Therefore, those few readers who may have read any of my previous books may recognize some of the stories. I hope they will be greeted as old friends rather than redundant bores.

CHAPTER TWO

Objectives

Problem solving, as we have seen, involves the selection of one or more courses of action (means) in the pursuit of one or more objectives (ends). An objective is a desired outcome. Knowing what our objectives are is clearly important in problem solving. If others are involved in our problem (and they usually are), it is also important to know their relevant objectives. Finally, it is also clearly of value to understand how their objectives and ours are related. In this chapter, we consider how problem solving can be improved by a better understanding of (1) our own objectives, (2) those of the others involved, and (3) how their and our objectives are related.

OUR OWN OBJECTIVES

Problems are of two types: those involving the destruction, removal, or containment of something that is present but not desired, and those involving the acquisition or attainment of something that is absent but desired. The first type of problem, one that is *negatively* oriented, is concerned with eliminating a source of dissatisfaction, for example, a distracting noise, an illness, or a debt. The second type, one that is *positively* oriented, is concerned with attaining access to a source of satisfaction, for example, a friend, a good book, or money.

Positive and negative—applied to objectives—appear to be relative concepts. For example, the desire to get rid of noise may be stated as the desire to obtain quiet and the desire to cure an illness as the desire to obtain health. However, one should be wary of such glib equating.

If one does not want to hear the music being played on the radio, getting rid of it is a negative objective. If one wants to hear a different type of music, this is a positive objective. Note that this positive objective implies the attainment of one that is negative, *but the converse is not true.* In most cases, getting rid of what one does not want is *not* equivalent to obtaining what one does want.

The major difference between positive and negative objectives, however, is not logical but psychological. We explore this difference later.

Although positive and negative are not completely relative concepts, "ends" and "means" are. Every means can also be considered to be an end, and every end a means. For example, buying an automobile can be considered a means for obtaining personal transportation, an end. Personal transportation can be considered to be a means for getting to work, an end. Getting to work is a means for obtaining income, and so on. Every less-than-ultimate end can be considered a means to a more ultimate end.

The car-purchasing example also shows that every means can be considered an end. The first means in the example, buying a car, can be considered the end of going to the dealer. Going to the dealer can be considered the end of borrowing a friend's car, and so on.

That every means is an end can be seen in another way. It was pointed out previously that decision makers are concerned with the efficiencies of available means for possible outcomes. The efficiency of a means for a desired outcome, an end, is, in most general terms, the probability that it will produce that end. The higher this probability, the more efficient the means. Thus the efficiency of a means is a measure of its *instrumental* or *extrinsic* value, its usefulness. The extrinsic value of anything lies in what it can be used for, its ability to bring about something else that is valued. For example, the extrinsic value of money lies in the value of what it can buy. For most of us money has virtually no other value. For coin collectors, however, certain types of money have values that are unrelated to what they can be used for, but are related to what they are in themselves.

If means (courses of action) and instruments used in them—such as money, tables, automobiles, language, and arithmetic—had only extrinsic value, decision makers would be indifferent to choices involving them when they are equally efficient for the same ends, but this is frequently not the case. For example, although each of a number of differently colored shirts, identical in every other respect, has the same efficiency as clothing as any of the others, we may nevertheless have preferences among them. We like some colors better than others; they are more satisfying. Thus the desire for a particular color shirt may be said to be an "end in itself." The value we place on the color is *intrinsic*, noninstrumental. Similarly, we prefer one symphony to another even though neither may be useful for anything. Intrinsic value derives from immediate satisfaction, extrinsic value from anticipated consequences.

The intrinsic values of means are seldom explicitly formulated. They are difficult to formulate because, among other things, a large number of them may be relevant in any situation. Furthermore, they are very personal values that are difficult or impossible to defend. The importance of such values and the difficulty of formulating them in advance are illustrated in the following fable.

Fable 2.1.   A FUNNY THING HAPPENED ON THE WAY TO THE FACTORY.

A small company that manufactured hand tools for carpentry was owned by three men who served as its president, vice president and financial officer, and vice president of operations. The former two were also presidents of two banks in the small community in which the company was located. They spent little time at the company. The vice president of operations was there more than the others but was seldom there more than half the time. The absence of the owner-executives was not due to lack of concern but to their recognition of the fact that the company could run itself quite well without their involvement.

The vice president of operations, in an effort to do something useful, began to play with some relevant numbers. He found that although the company's share of the market in which it operated had been increasing regularly for many years, the total volume of industry sales was declining. By looking ahead he could see that unless there was a significant change in demand for hand tools, the growth of his company could not continue.

He discussed this apprehension with his two fellow executives. Together they decided to play it safe by diversifying, by adding a product line that would enable the company to maintain its growth even if demand for carpentry tools continued to decrease. They called on Aesop and his colleagues for assistance in this effort.

Aesop and his team began by analyzing the company's operations to familiarize themselves with its production technology and modes of distribution and sales. Once this was completed they began a search for other products that required similar technology and modes of distribution and sales. The search was directed at finding a product that "fit" the company and whose sales were increasing.

The first one they found was obvious: tools used by plumbers. They presented this finding to the three executives hesitantly because they doubted that it had not already been considered. The executives said that, indeed, they had considered it but they had hoped for something "better." Aesop asked what "better" meant. The president said that he could not possibly define it but that when Aesop came up with an alternative that was "better" the executives would recognize it easily. He asked that the search continue.

Aesop took the search into more exotic tools and came up with those used in aircraft maintenance. When this was presented to the executives they expressed more, but not great, interest, and again they suggested that the search continue. When Aesop pressed for specification of the criteria they were using, he was put off again in the same way as before. The search was continued with several more repetitions of proposal and rejection.

On his way to a subsequent meeting with the executives, Aesop, listening to his car radio, heard a discussion of the significance of the then-recently-developed transistor. This gave him an outrageous idea. At the meeting with the executives he suggested that they go into the transistor business. The response was enthusiastic and was immediately followed by the question, "Can you tell us what a transistor is?"

In the subsequent discussion Aesop learned that the executives were looking for a challenge and an opportunity to get reinvolved in their business by the introduction of a new, not a familiar, technology. As one of the executives put it, "We'd like to get more fun out of the business and feel more a part of it."

Eventually, at the suggestion of Aesop and his colleagues, the company went into the hydraulic-coupling and valve business. The three executives lived happily ever after.

> **MORAL:** **One can enjoy a game played by others, but one can only have fun by playing it onself.**

Fun is a recreative, an aesthetic, objective. It derives from the intrinsic value of the means employed. It has nothing to do with efficiency or economics.

Important decisions, even in business, are often dominated by considerations that have little or nothing to do with efficiency or economics. For example, a major corporation's profits were suffering because of its commitment to producing only the highest quality products in its field. Its material costs were inflating more rapidly than those of its competitors, but it refused to abort its products or abbreviate the processes by which they were made, as its competitors did. To have degraded its product would have significantly reduced the satisfaction its managers derived from their work. This had to do with the intrinsic value of work, a means.

Another case: there are two districts of the Federal Reserve banking system that have exactly the same functions but differ significantly in the way they are organized and operate. The "atmospheres" in these two banks are entirely different. The difference cannot be explained in terms of efficiency; both are efficient. The differences are a matter of *style,* and style has to do with the intrinsic value of means.

Each means preference based on intrinsic value is an aspect of an individual's or group's style. Persistent stylistic preferences are called *traits,* for example, ascendant-submissive, introverted-extroverted, aggressive, sociable, charitable, courageous, apathetic, and so on. (G. W. Allport and H. S. Odbert, in 1936, identified 17,953 trait names in English.) The set of traits that characterizes each of us constitutes our *style.* Our individuality, our uniqueness, lies at least as much in our style as it does in the ends we pursue.

Style has to do with the satisfaction we derive from *what* we do, rather than what we do it *for.*

A reduction in the satisfaction of stylistic objectives is partially responsible for the current deterioration of the quality of life. Less and less satisfaction is derived from the ordinary things we do such as taking a walk or drive, attending school, or working. This decrease in satisfaction is a consequence of a reduction in the aesthetic properties of our environment and what we do within it. Alienation from work, which results from a reduced quality of work life, is a special case of the dissatisfaction produced by activity that has little or no intrinsic value.

Now consider ends that, as mentioned, can also be looked at as means. They have extrinsic (instrumental) value as well as intrinsic value. Their extrinsic value lies in their consequences. The failure to consider ends as means and, therefore, their likely consequences, can itself have serious consequences. The following fable illustrates the point.

Fable 2.2.   DANGER! GRADE TOSSING.

The undergraduates at a large American university had carried out an organized protest against the institution's conventional grading system over an extended period of time. The intensity of the protest increased to a point at which it could no longer be ignored. The university's administration responded by appointing a faculty committee to review the grading system. The committee eventually issued recommendations for minor changes that were overwhelmingly rejected by both faculty and students, but for different reasons. The students then demanded to be given a voice in redesigning the system. A new committee was formed that gave the students token representation.

The second committee's recommendations were no better received than those made earlier. The students' protest intensified and rapidly approached disruptive behavior when the now-desperate administration told the student body it could select its own committee to generate recommendations to be presented to the faculty and students for approval.

An all-student committee was quickly selected and convened. At the opening of its first meeting one of its members moved that the committee recommend the elimination of grades. After a short discussion the motion was passed.

The committee's chairman then suggested that a defense of the recommendation be developed and submitted with it. The others agreed. A discussion of the nature of the defense was initiated. After several suggestions had been made, one student suggested that the committee determine what would happen when he and others applied to another university for admission to its graduate school and could provide no grades. The others agreed that this should be investigated. The chairman asked each member of the committee to make the necessary inquiries of one graduate school that he designated and to be prepared to report back at the next meeting.

The second meeting opened with reports of the inquiries. They were uniform: students without grades would not be admitted to any of the graduate schools that had been contacted. The committee was dejected but eventually rallied. First, it withdrew its previously passed motion to recommend elimination of grades. Second, it began a serious discussion directed at finding what was objectionable in the grading system. This discussion carried through a series of meetings.

Two deficiencies were identified, and remedies were found for each. First, the students objected to the competitiveness bred by the disclosure of grades to peers. Therefore, they recommended that information on student grades not be disseminated to anyone other than the student without his permission. Second, they felt that concern over grades constrained their exploring areas of interest by taking courses in which they feared their performance might not be as good as they would like. Therefore, they recommended that each student be allowed to take one course of his choice each semester on a simple pass–fail basis.

Both recommendations were overwhelmingly accepted by the faculty and the student body.

> **MORAL: The end of one problem may be the beginning of another.**

The outcome of a problem's solution can always be considered as a means to more ultimate consequences. Therefore, to determine the extrinsic value of any less-than-ultimate outcome, we should know what outcome we ultimately want and how close to it the immediate outcome brings us.

Ultimately desired outcomes are the only ones that can have purely intrinsic value because they have no consequences. They must be unattainable but approachable. If they were not approachable, they would have no effect on our current behavior. Their approachability makes *progress* toward them the relevant measure of the extrinsic value of any less-than-ultimate outcome.

An ultimately desired outcome is called an *ideal*. Omniscience, for example, has been said to be an ideal of science. We can never know everything, but we can always know more. An ideal of some, to take another example, is to move with infinite speed. No one will ever be able to do so, but increased speed is always possible.

The lack of a sense of progress toward ideals, the growing belief that much of the rapid cultural and technological change is getting us nowhere, is another major contributor to a decreasing quality of life. A sense of progress toward ideals gives life meaning and makes choice significant. Today more and more people feel that they are no longer in control of their futures. This tends to make them view their choices as illusory rather than real. Fatalism and resignation to a future that is out of our control degrades the quality of our lives. In contrast, the belief that the future depends on what *we* do between now and then enhances this quality.

It is apparent that what we want, our ends, influences our choice of means. Not so apparent is the fact that the available means influence our choice of ends. Our conception of possible outcomes affects what outcomes we desire. Our ability to solve problems is thereby limited by our conception of what is feasible. Furthermore, even our conception of the nature of the problem may be limited in this way. However, such limits are often self-imposed.

Many of our problems derive from a dissatisfaction with some aspect of our current state. For example, we do not like the way our car is working, how sales are going, the cost of materials, and so on. As noted above, many of our problem formulations are directed at getting rid of what we do not want. We tend to be moved more by our dislikes than our likes, more by our hates than our loves. The effort to get rid of what we do not want is *reactive*, retrospectively oriented problem solving. The effort to obtain what we want is *proactive*, prospectively oriented problem solving. In reactive problem solving we walk into the future facing the past—we move away from, rather than toward, something. This often results in unforseen consequences that are more distasteful than the deficiencies removed. Recall the students' grading problem. The consequences of D.D.T. provide another example.

In proactive problem solving we specify where we want to go, and we try to get there. Although such an approach does not eliminate the possibility of overlooking relevant consequences of our solutions, it reduces the probability of doing so. The more ultimate the desired outcome we specify, the more likely we are to consider the intermediate and long-run consequences of our immediate actions. The more immediate the source of dissatisfaction we try to get rid of, the less likely we are to take account of relevant consequences. Therefore, *the chances of overlooking relevant consequences are minimized when we formulate a problem in terms of approaching one or more ideals.*

When we focus on the deficiencies of our current state, we tend to view each deficiency independently. Thus viewed, many deficiencies appear difficult to remove. Because focusing on an ideal reveals the relationships between different things that can be done in the future, it tends to make us deal simultaneously with sets of interacting threats and opportunities, to treat them as a whole, as a *system of problems*. The effort to deal with sets of interacting problems as a whole is what *planning*, in contrast to problem solving, should be about.

Planning implies not only dealing holistically with a number of interacting problems, but also doing so with a prospective orientation. Unfortunately, much of what is called planning is preoccupied with correcting a number of independently perceived deficiencies.

Proactive problem solving is always imbedded in a planning process. No problem is treated in isolation, but each problem is formulated as one of a set of interrelated problems that is treated as a whole. *Proactive planning consists of designing a desirable future and finding ways of moving toward it as effectively as possible.*

The design of a desirable future is best carried out when it is imbedded in an *idealized redesign* of whatever is being planned for—a nation, an agency, a business, a group, or an individual. Such a redesign is an explicit statement of what the designers would have *now* if they could have whatever they wanted. Such design should be subjected to only two constraints. First, the design should be technologically feasible. This does not preclude technological innovation; it is intended to prevent the process from becoming an exercise in science fiction. It would be permissible, for example, to include office-to-office color facsimile transmission or the use of helicopters for urban transportation because these are technologically feasible. However, one should not assume telepathic communications between home and office.

All other types of externally imposed constraint—for example, economic, political, and legal—should be disregarded.

The second constraint is that the thing or state designed should be so designed that if it were brought into existence, it could survive. The design should be operationally viable.

In addition, of course, any design is unavoidably constrained by its designers' lack of information, knowledge, understanding, and wisdom, not to mention imagination. Thus an idealized state of affairs should be one in which its designers would be capable of both learning from their experience in it and adapting to changes in themselves and their environment. It follows that an ideal system or state should be flexible and capable of being changed easily so that it can be improved continually.

An idealized design is not utopian precisely because it is capable of being improved. It is the best its designers can conceptualize *now,* but its design, unlike that of a utopia, is based on a recognition of the fact that *no idealized design can remain ideal for long.* Thus the product of an idealized design is not an ideal state or system, but an *ideal-seeking* state or system.

An idealized design is not utopian for another reason. Its designers need not pretend to have the final answers to all questions that can be asked about the ideal. Where they do not have an answer, they should design into the state a capability of finding it. Such a design is never completed and is never absolute, final, or fixed. It is subject to continual revision in light of newly acquired information, knowledge, understanding, wisdom, and imagination.

Idealized design has been used in a variety of contexts. The research unit of which I am a part recently collaborated with the government of France in the preparation of an idealized design of Paris (Roles et Fonctions . . . , 1973). This design has since been adopted as the basis of that city's long-range planning. A similar effort is being initiated for

Mexico City. This research unit has also been involved in an idealized redesign of a district of the Federal Reserve System. A short time ago it participated in an idealized redesign of our nation's juvenile justice system (Management and Behavioral Science Center, 1972). It has also participated in such redesigns of several corporations in the United States and abroad. It recently completed an idealized design of our nation's Scientific Communication and Technology Transfer System (R. L. Ackoff et al., 1976). A companion effort is being carried out in Mexico at CONACYT, the National Science Foundation of that country. A number of my own idealized redesigns appears in my book *Redesigning the Future* (R. L. Ackoff, 1974). A brief description of the design of the National Scientific Communication and Technology Transfer System is given in Chapter 6.

Idealized design is as applicable to small systems, even individuals, as it is to large ones; it is as applicable to parts of a system as it is to the whole.

The idealized design process unleashes creativity because it relaxes internally imposed constraints. It sanctions imaginative irreverence for things as they are and encourages exploration of areas previously precluded by self-imposed and culturally imposed taboos. For example, a group that was trying to produce an idealized redesign of our nation's banking system began one of its discussions by expressing the desire to eliminate the use of checks in such a system because of the increasingly unmanageable burden of clearing them. One of the members of the group pointed out that this would be possible if there were an integrated National Electronic Funds Transfer System. Such a system would enable anyone to transfer funds from his bank account to that of another instantaneously without the use of paper. A second member of the group pointed out that one of the principal uses of checks was for paying salaries, dividends, and so on. He suggested, therefore, that in an idealized system all payments to an individual or organization be made electronically. Another member of the group pointed out that if the total incomes of every person and organization were received electronically, it would be possible for banks to prepare tax returns on computers. If a bank had a record of all income, it would also have a complete record of all expenditures. It was then pointed out that such a system would work only if every person had only one bank account, or, if he had multiple accounts, they all used his social security number for identification.

At this point one member of the group broke out with: "Wait a minute! If we had a complete record of all expenditures, wouldn't it make more sense to tax consumption than income?" This unleashed an excited exploration of the idea. Eventually it led to the design of a new tax system that all present thought was superior to the one we had. They felt that, although their design was currently infeasible for political reasons, it should be pushed for over the long run. Later they learned that just such efforts were being made in Sweden and England.

An individual's concept of what is feasible is one of the principal self-imposed constraints on problem solving and planning. Here is a case in point.

While on a recent sabbatical leave in Mexico City I met with a group of planners who were addressing the transportation problems of that city. They reviewed for me each of the alternatives they were considering in their efforts to improve the transportation system. None of them, I said, seemed to me to be able to significantly improve that system. They challenged me to identify alternatives that would, in my opinion, make a significant difference. I mentioned a number including the following three.

First, by redesigning the automobile. The people-carrying capacity of city streets can be increased by as much as 500 percent by the use of a rational "urmobile" (R. L. Ackoff, 1974, Chapter 11).

Second, by changing the work week to include five nine-hour days with no more than one hour off for lunch. During the current two- to three-hour midday break, most Mexicans return home for their meals. This almost doubles the transportation requirement.

Third, dispersing the federal government, locating most of it outside Mexico City. This would have a number of advantages in addition to reducing transportation requirements.

The planners responded by saying that none of these suggestions was feasible. The reasons they gave were political. Politics has been defined as the art of the possible. The possible, as conceived by most politicians and those who serve them, is seldom enough to solve the important problems in hand. What they consider impossible is required to solve these problems. This is where planning and problem solving *should* help. Politicians should employ *the art and science of the impossible*—of making the apparently impossible possible. To practice planning or problem solving as the art of the possible is to play politics and call it something else. It deceives those engaged in it as well as those affected by it.

To convert the apparently impossible into the possible, it is necessary to remove or relax constraints that derive from considering feasibility. Idealized design can be extremely effective in removing and relaxing such constraints.

In idealized design, as in all design, parts are assembled into a whole. Design is essentially a synthesizing process. Its product is always a system, a set of interrelated parts that form a whole. Design, particularly idealized design, focuses on the properties of the whole.

A system always has properties that its parts lack. For example, a person can read, write, run, and make love, but no part or subset of parts of a person can do these things. Thus a system of solutions to interrelated problems always has properties that its parts lack, and its parts acquire properties by being a part of that system that they would not otherwise have. For example, a citizen has rights in the nation of which he is a part that a noncitizen does not have. Therefore, a plan—which is a system of solutions to a system of problems—can be feasible *even if none of its parts are feasible when considered separately.* Solutions that are infeasible can interact separately to yield a feasible system of solutions.

For example, as a result of the idealized redesign of Paris, an important body in the French government has accepted two recommendations that, when considered separately and out of the context of the idealized design, hardly seem feasible. They are (1) that the capital of France be moved from Paris and (2) that Paris eventually be made a self-governing open city. These recommendations were accepted because they were necessary to pursue the "ideal": Paris as the (informal) capital of the world. Clearly, if Paris is to play such a role, it cannot simultaneously serve as capital of a nation, nor can any nation have sovereignty over it. It must "belong" to the world.

In the discussion that followed a presentation of the National Scientific Comunication and Technology Transfer System to a large conference of information scientists, one young man said, "I think the design is great, but I don't see why you call it ideal. There is nothing in the design that we could not have now if we really wanted it." That young man got the point: *the principal obstruction between man and the future he desires is man.* The product of idealized design makes this apparent. Therefore, this design process is a powerful means of converting the apparently impossible to the possible. Moreover, an idealized design is also capable of mobilizing a collective effort to obtain it. Designs produced by the idealization process are often *mobilizing ideas,* ones that extract commitments to pursue the apparently impossible. The reason for this are not obscure.

First, idealized design facilitates the widespread participation of all those who are potentially affected by the product of the design. The process requires no special skill; anyone can participate. It is usually fun to participate, and those engaged in the process have a chance to think deeply and learn about a system that is important to them. *It en-*

*ables them to become conscious of and express their stylistic prefer-
ences and ideals.*

Not all those who have a stake in a system comprehend it equally
well or in equal detail or scope; however, participants in idealized design need only involve themselves initially with those aspects of the
system which are interesting to them. Interactions with other participants make all those involved conscious of the potential effects of their
design of a part of the system on other parts of the system and on the
system as a whole. This enables them to increase their understanding
of the system, to *learn,* and this is personal development.

Second, idealization tends to generate consensus among those involved. This follows from the fact that it focuses on ultimate values,
and there is generally less disagreement about such values than about
shorter-run objectives and the means for pursuing them. For example,
the constitutions of the Soviet Union and the United States are very
much alike. Most disagreements between these two nations derive
from differences over means, not ends.

When explicit agreement is reached on ultimate values, differences
over shorter-range objectives and means are more easily resolved. Furthermore, where differences cannot be resolved, experiments can and
should be designed into the system to resolve them.

Before leaving the subject of idealized design, a short exercise may
reveal more about it.

At the end of this sentence *stop reading* and list all the deficiencies
you can think of that relate to the current telephone system.

Put your list aside for a moment. Now suppose you could have any
type of technologically feasible telephone system you wanted. List some
of the more important properties it would have. *Stop. Make your list.*

Here are a few of the properties my ideal telephone system would
have.

1. I would be able to use a telephone without using my hands.

2. I would be able to use it from any location in which I happened to be.

3. I would not receive any "wrong numbers."

4. When a call came for me I would be informed who was calling
before I answered the phone and therefore would not have to answer when so inclined.

5. When I was speaking on the phone and another party was trying to reach me, I would be informed who it was and I would be
able to put him on "hold" or take a message. If I were the caller I
would not have to hang on but could be called back automatically

when the party was free, provided he was disposed to receive my call.

6. I would be able to leave messages for specific callers when I was not available to receive their calls.

7. I would be able to hold conference calls as easily as two-party calls.

8. The option of visual as well as auditory communication would always be available.

My friends in telecommunications tell me that all this is technologically feasible.

Compare your second list with mine. Chances are they overlap considerably. Now compare your first and second lists. Which would yield a better system? Chances are the second would because you considered improvements that were not implied by your list of deficiencies. This, of course, is one of the points of the exercise.

Idealized design is not all there is to either problem solving or planning, but it is the best way I know of to open and stimulate the mind to creative activity. Furthermore, it is the best way I know of finding out what one's objectives really are.

THE OBJECTIVES OF OTHERS

The solutions to most personal problems—let alone group, organizational, or societal problems—affect others as well as the problem solver. The others generally react to any solution that is proposed or implemented. Their reactions are determined by how the solution affects the pursuit of their objectives. It is necessary to understand their objectives if one is to correctly anticipate their responses and, therefore, the consequences of a solution.

Those who have authority over others generally assume they understand the others and know their objectives. They are frequently wrong. Nevertheless, when unexpected and unintended consequences follow the implementation of a solution because of this type of error, those who made the error seldom question their understanding of others. Rather, the unexpected consequences are rationalized by attributing irrationality to the others. Whatever else such rationalization may do, it provides no better understanding of the others and thus does not lead to better solutions. It generally induces a resigned acceptance of ineffectiveness.

The next three fables illustrate this point.

**Fable 2.3.   CONTRACEPTION MAY BE A
MISCONCEPTION.**

In 1957 Aesop spent some time in India at the invitation of its government to review its national development-planning procedures. While
there he met a number of foreigners who were trying to introduce
family planning to India in the hope of bringing its population explo-
sion under control. Most of these serious and dedicated people were

**Fable 2.3. Contraception may be a misconception. Moral: Irrationality is
usually in the mind of the beholder, not in the mind of the beheld.**

distributing contraceptives and information about their use, but they were not succeeding. They had had little impact on India's birth rate. They blamed their failure on the ignorance, irrationality, or intransigence of the Indians. Such an explanation of their failure yielded no ideas about how to increase effectiveness.

Aesop suggested to some of them that they consider the assumption that the Indians were rational and they were not. This, he argued, might yield a more useful explanation of their failure. Furthermore, he pointed out, there was at least some evidence that another of their basic assumptions—that the Indians did not know how to control family size—was wrong. Indian families tended to have considerably less than the twenty to thirty children it was biologically possible for them to have. This suggested that they were already practicing considerable birth control. Granting this, the problem seemed to be one of determining why they *wanted* as many children as they had. This was quite at odds with assuming, as the family planners did, that the number of children Indians had was out of their control.

None of the family planners to whom Aesop made these suggestions took the bait. Eventually, Aesop himself did. This is what he found.

After obtaining its independence, India had increased the expected length of life of adults dramatically, but it had not increased the span of *employable* life. The poor Indian—and most of them are poor—could expect to work for only about the first half of the employable years available to him. Therefore, while young and employed, Indians were preoccupied with planning for financial security during the subsequent period of unemployment.

The Indian government provided no unemployment insurance or old-age security. Very few Indians earned enough to insure themselves. Therefore, the only way most Indians could assure survival was by having enough children to support the husband and wife when the husband was unemployable. On the average, one wage earner could provide the minimal support required by one non-wage-earning adult. However, since only males are generally employable in India, this implied a need for an average of four children. Because of the high mortality rate among children, slightly more than four children were required to produce four who would survive. The average family size in India corresponded almost exactly to this requirement.

The average size of families in India could, of course, have been due to other factors. Whether it was, however, could be easily determined. If the security-based explanation of family size was correct, one would expect those couples whose first two or three children were sons to be smaller than those whose first few children were daughters. This was found to be the case.

Aesop did not claim that concern with advanced-age unemployment was the only factor affecting birth rate in India, but that it was a critical factor. Therefore, to ask Indians to have fewer children was to ask them to commit a delayed suicide. To call them irrational because they refused to do so is hardly rational.

> **MORAL: Irrationality is usually in the mind of the beholder, not in the mind of the beheld.**

Misunderstanding the objectives of others is common where there is a cultural gap separating the problem solver and those affected by the solution. It should be kept in mind that cultural gaps exist *within* societies as well as between them. Here is a case in point.

Fable 2.4.   WELL READ CAN WELL MEAN DEAD.

The leaders of a Black ghetto on the border of a city university considered illiteracy to be a major problem in their neighborhood. They started a primary school to which they invited experts on reading problems to help them teach reading to children. Program after program developed by the experts failed to produce significant results. The experts concluded that the children were uneducable. At this point Aesop and his colleagues were asked for assistance.

Aesop began by assuming that the children were rational and therefore that the experts were not. Using this assumption he sought an explanation for the rejection of reading by the young Blacks. It was not hard to find.

First, he learned that most homes in the ghetto contained no books other than the telephone book. Therefore, most children seldom or never saw their parents read and seldom or never were read to. Since these children, like most, idolized their parents, who obviously placed no value on reading, the children did likewise. Furthermore, a youth carrying books openly on the ghetto's streets invited abuse, often physical, by his peers. He was not only considered to be a sissy but also to have accepted "Whitey's" values.

When a child reared in such an environment entered school, he or she was immediately confronted by a stranger, usually white, who acted as though reading were the most important thing in the world. Any wonder the child rejected it?

Fable 2.4. Well read can well mean dead. Moral: What appears to be black on white to Whites may appear to be all white to Blacks.

Aesop devoted his efforts to trying to find a way to make the children *want* to read. He found several ways of doing so. In one, a number of silent films that had been made for children's matinees in the nineteen twenties were shown continually in the school's auditorium. Any child was permitted to watch them whenever he or she wanted to. To understand them, however, it was necessary to be able to read the subtitles. This provided the necessary motivation to many of the children, and they began to learn how to read.

MORAL: What appears to be black on white to
          Whites may appear to be all white to
          Blacks.

Much of this book was written while I was spending a sabbatical year
doing research and teaching in Mexico. In Mexico I ran across the following example of "we-they" intracultural misunderstanding.

Fable 2.5.   THOSE WHO GIVE A DAM MAY
NOT BE WELL RECEIVED.

A Mexican government agency responsible for the development of
water resources decided to build a dam and use it to irrigate a large
farming area the productivity of which, it believed, could thereby be
doubled. When the agency's plans were completed, it sent representatives to the rural areas that would be affected to explain the project to
the peasants and to determine whether they wanted it. The answers
were uniformly "yes."

The dam and irrigation system were built at great expense but failed
to produce the expected increase in productivity of the land. The puzzled experts went out to determine why. They found that the peasants
had reduced the amount of land under cultivation, thereby obtaining
more time to work in nearby towns or do nothing. They felt that the
amount of work required to use all their land was not justified by the
small increase in their income that it would bring about.

"Why," one of the experts asked a consultant, "didn't they tell us
this before we built the dam?" The consultant could have replied: "Because you didn't ask the right questions. You incorrectly assumed you
knew the answers." But he did not. Instead he asked the expert if he
played the violin. The puzzled expert answered negatively. Then the
consultant asked him what he would do if he were offered a Stradi-
varius. He said he would accept it. The consultant asked him why since
he could not play it. The expert got the point.

MORAL: The reason for one person's giving may
          not be the reason for another's receiving.

The cultural gap that keeps problem solvers from understanding the
objectives of others can occur even within relatively small and apparently homogeneous organizations. An example is provided in Fable 3.4.

In problems the solutions to which involve the reactions of others,

Fable 2.5. Those who give a dam may not be well received. Moral: The reason for one person's giving may not be the reason for another's receiving.

their *participation* in the problem-solving process is the best protection against unexpected responses. Where we fail to obtain such participation because we perceive the others as being in conflict with us, we virtually assure continuation of the conflict if it exists. A failure to consult others who have a stake in our decisions is often seen as an act of aggression, because it often is. An invitation to participation in decision making is an act of conciliation, a demonstration of care and concern.

THE RELATIONSHIP BETWEEN THE OBJECTIVES
OF TWO OR MORE PARTIES

One party is in *conflict* with another if the action of the first party has an effect on the outcome of the action of the second, and this effect is to reduce the value of the outcome to the second party. If, on the other hand, the effect of the action of the first party is an increase in the value of the outcome of the second's behavior, the first *cooperates* with the second. If the first party's behavior has no effect on that of the second, the second is *independent* of the first.

These relationships are not necessarily symmetrical; for example, one party may cooperate with a second while the second conflicts with the first. The master–slave relationship is an extreme case of this. Where conflict or cooperation is not symmetrical, the one who benefits most or suffers least is said to *exploit* the other. Exploitation need not be deliberate or conscious.

Competition is frequently defined as "conflict according to rules" or "constrained conflict." These definitions do not capture the essential property of competition. In competition two or more parties are in conflict with each other relative to one or more objectives of each, but this conflict efficiently serves another objective of either the conflicting parties or another party. For example, the opponents in a tennis match are in conflict with respect to winning, but this conflict is efficient relative to the recreational objective they share. They cooperate with respect to recreation. In economic competition the companies involved are in conflict with respect to their desire for sales, but such conflict is supposed to serve efficiently the interests of consumers by providing them with better services at a lower price than they would otherwise enjoy.

Laws, regulations, and rules that govern competition are intended to ensure the effectiveness of the conflict involved for the "cooperative" objective. In the American economic system, for example, price fixing is precluded because this is believed to be detrimental to the interests of the consumers. Similarly, the rules of tennis, or any other game, are intended to ensure their recreational value for either the participants taken collectively, or their spectators, or both.

There are three ways of dealing with conflict, and these correspond to the ways of dealing with problems in general: *solution, resolution,* and *dissolution.*

To attempt to *solve* a conflict of which one is a part—whether or not it is imbedded in competition—is to accept the conditions that produce the conflict and to seek a way of getting what one wants, whatever the cost to the opponent. Therefore, to try to solve a conflict is to try to *win* it. This may be done with or without the use of force. To try to win without the use of force has come to be called "gamesmanship." To use force is to *fight*. In a fight one or both opponents try to eliminate, remove, incapacitate, or inactivate the other—to overcome him. A fight may be avoided or discontinued by submission or surrender of one of the parties. Fights may be prevented or stopped by the forceful intervention, or threat of such intervention, by a third party, usually stronger than the opponents.

Efforts to solve a conflict generally intensify it until one party defeats the other. Therefore, solutions frequently create conditions that breed future conflict, and subsequent conflicts are often more intense. Conflicts that are deterred by force or threats of force also tend to intensify over time.

To attempt to *resolve* a conflict is to accept the conditions that create it and to seek a compromise, a distribution of gains and/or losses that is acceptable to the participants. Each party usually gives up something it wanted but obtains something it might not otherwise have obtained. Agreement on a settlement is normally reached when the participants feel that the proposed distribution of gains and losses is *fair*—that is, it eliminates or reduces exploitation.

Negotiation, bargaining, and arbitration are common processes by which resolutions to conflicts are sought.

The *theory of games* is a body of scientific knowledge developed since World War II that is applicable to the search for settlements. Resolving settlements usually stabilize conflict, but they seldom deintensify them as dissolution can.

To *dissolve* a conflict, the conditions that produce it are changed so that it disappears. This can be done by changing either the environment or the opponents.

Many conflicts are a consequence of scarcity. Two children want to play with the same toy, the only one of its kind in the environment. Two adults want the last remaining parking space in a lot. Such conflicts can sometimes be dissolved by removing the scarcity, for example, making another toy or parking space available.

Some conflicts are based on an invasion of the senses. For example, one person wants to read in a quiet room in which another wants to listen to blaring music. Such conflicts can sometimes be dissolved by "dividing" the environment. For example, a pair of earphones might allow one to hear music at whatever volume he desires while the other reads in peace. A physical division of the environment can sometimes accomplish the same result, for example, the use of a curtain to block an annoying light turned on by another, or closing a door to shut out a noise. In dissolution of conflict neither party loses; both get what they want without compromise.

Not all conflicts result from a clash of objectives that have been chosen freely, particularly conflicts that arise between parts of the same organization. Such conflicts are often imposed on the opponents by a third party who has some control over both of them. Conflicts of this type are often unintentional. Here is a case in point.

Fable 2.6. IT'S HARD TO SELL WHAT ONE DOES NOT HAVE.

This is a story about a chain of department stores that bought and sold a wide variety of products. Since the number of items handled has no relevance to the story I tell it as though only one product were involved.

The two basic operations of department stores are, of course, buying from suppliers and selling to customers. These were handled in this case by a purchasing department and a merchandizing department. The objective given to the purchasing department by the chain's executive officer was to minimize the average size of inventory while meeting expected demand. Therefore, the most critical variables controlled by the purchasing department were the size and frequency of purchases.

The objective assigned to the merchandizing department was to maximize gross profit: (number of items sold) times (selling price minus purchase price). Its principal controlled variable was selling price.

The merchandizing department had a statistical section that plotted the number of items sold against selling price in each period. This yielded a price-demand curve such as the one shown in Figure 2.1. The top "optimistic" line represented the largest number of the item that the store could reasonably expect to sell. The middle "realistic" line represented the "expected" or "average" amount sold at each price. The lower "pessimistic" line represented the smallest amount the store could expect to sell. (The upper and lower lines were drawn so that the probability of going above the top or below the bottom was 0.05.)

The merchandizing manager—let's call him Mike—would decide what price to charge for the item some time in advance. Suppose he selected price P_1 shown in Figure 2.2. He then had to decide how many of the item he would like to have in stock at the appropriate time. Using Figure 2.2 he selected quantity Q_1 to be sure that he would not run out of stock. If he ran out of stock, his measure of performance would

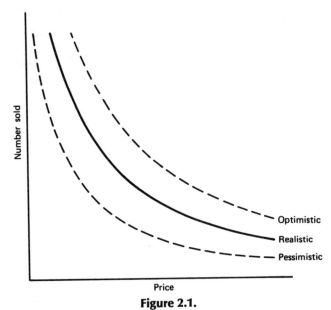

Figure 2.1.

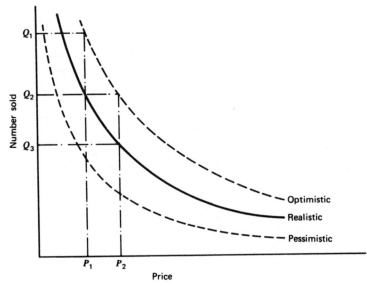

Figure 2.2.

suffer. Having made this decision he notified Pat, the purchasing manager, of his desire for Q_1 of the item at the specified time.

Now Pat was the former assistant merchandizing manager; he also had a copy of Figure 2.2, and he knew how Mike had selected Q_1. Pat consulted the figure and decided to order only quantity Q_2, the expected number of sales at price P_1. He wanted to avoid being overstocked because this would hurt his performance.

Mike, however, knew that Pat would do this so he really intended to charge price P_2 which would maximize his expected gross profit if only Q_2 were available. Pat, on the other hand, knew Mike would go to price P_2; therefore he intended to order only Q_3, the expected number of sales at price P_2. But Mike knew that Pat would do this . . . and so on. The limit of this process would have been reached when nothing was bought and therefore nothing was sold. The limit was not reached because the two managers were not allowed to communicate with each other. Each had to guess what the other would try to do. Although this hardly made for optimal operations, it made survival possible.

> **MORAL:** Every gain of control over others is a potential loss of control over oneself.

The conflict between the two departments was imposed on them through their assigned objectives. Their performance and the store's as a whole was subsequently improved by changing these objectives to dissolve the conflict. The cost to be minimized by the purchasing department was modified to include the cost of lost sales. The merchandizing department, on the other hand, was charged with the cost of carrying inventory in excess of expected demand.

Here is a similar situation in a very different context.

Fable 2.7. PUTTING THE TOP IN THE MIDDLE.

A large diversified company had two relatively autonomous divisions one of which produced and sold a product of which the second was a user. A corporate policy required the second division to buy the product from the first and the first to supply the second. This led to intense conflict between the two divisions. The buying division could often buy the product for less from other suppliers, and the selling division could often sell its product to others for more than the buying division was willing to pay. The appropriate corporate executive was frequently called on to resolve the interdivisional dispute, but he could seldom find a way of doing so that would satisfy both divisions. This led to further intensification of the conflict.

Aesop was called on for help. By changing the rules imposed on the divisions, he was able to dissolve the conflict.

The buying division was made free to buy from the lowest-cost supplier even if it were outside the company *unless* the responsible corporate executive wanted the purchase to be made internally. If he did, he had to compensate the buying division for the difference between the inside and outside prices. When the buying division was willing to pay the supplying division's asking price, the supplying division had to sell to it. When the supplying division's asking price was lower than that of any other supplier, the buying division had to buy from it and pay the difference between the internal price and the lowest available external price to the responsible corporate executive.

This arrangement made a profit center of the responsible executive. It was now his responsibility to determine whether subsidized internal transfers of the product were worth their cost to the corporation.

MORAL: An internal conflict cannot be solved by imposing it on others.

It is not uncommon for a third party to try to resolve an internal conflict by setting up an apparently competitive situation between two other parties over which it has authority. This usually results in the conflict being given back to the third party in an intensified form. This was clearly the case in the previous two fables.

Now consider how the participants in a conflict may be changed so as to dissolve the conflict. We have already discussed one way of doing so: involving the opponents in an idealized-design process. This directs attention to ultimate objectives where there tends to be less disagreement than on intermediate or immediate objectives. The recognition of common ultimate objectives converts conflicts on less-than-ultimate objectives into questions about the efficiency of means, and these are dealt with more easily than ends conflicts.

Some conflicts can be dissolved by changing the values of one or more of the opponents through persuasion. A parent, for example, often tries to divert a child in conflict with another child by interesting him in something else. Adults are generally more difficult to divert, but it is not impossible to do so.

Informal discussion or formal debate between opponents is sometimes used to bring about their agreement. Only recently has much attention been given to the design of debates to increase their effectiveness as a means of dissolving conflicts. Professor Anatol Rapoport, in his book *Fights, Games, and Debates* (1960), has done a great deal to focus attention on the potential power of debates in dissolving conflicts. The debating procedure suggested here is an extension of the one proposed in his book. The procedure consists of the following steps.

1. Each participant should listen to the other express his views until he feels he can formulate the other's position in a way that is acceptable *to the other*. Each participant then attempts to do so. If the effort of either participant is unacceptable to the other, the discussion continues until both succeed.

If one of the parties wants to maintain a current state—for example, to retain capital punishment where it is used—he should be the first to attempt to formulate the other's position. If both seek change, the choice of who comes first should be made by chance. For example, if one participant wants to abolish capital punishment and his opponent wants to maintain it, the latter should make the first effort to state satisfactorily the position of the other. The reason for this is that the one who wants to maintain a current position is less likely to understand the other than the other is to understand him. As Ambrose Bierce (1911) once observed: "There is but one way to do nothing and diverse ways to do something . . ." (p. 159).

In some cases the first step may be enough to produce agreement. In other cases additional steps are required.

2. Once each participant can state the other's position to the other's satisfaction, each should formulate the factual and/or moral conditions under which he believes the other's position would be valid.

For example, in a dispute over capital punishment, the one who is opposed to it should state the conditions under which he believes it would be justified. He might say, "I believe capital punishment would be justified if it prevented more capital crimes than there were executions produced by it." Such a statement identifies "dissolving conditions" and makes it possible to convert many conflicts into questions of fact, for example, does capital punishment reduce the total number of lives taken?

On occasion one party may argue that the other's position is not justified under *any* conditions, for example, that capital punishment cannot be justified under any conditions. In this case the one who so argues should be called on to propose a method for resolving differences between two parties who hold opposite unconditional beliefs. If he does so and his opponent accepts it, the proposed procedure would then be used. If the proposed procedure is not acceptable to the opponent, the proposal becomes the subject of a debate using the procedure described here.

> 3. Once dissolving conditions have been agreed to, each participant should formulate his concept of how the *actual* conditions can be determined.

They may agree on these conditions. For example, they may agree to examine four classes of states over the last ten years: (1) states that have used capital punishment continually over this period, (2) those which have changed from no capital punishment to its use, (3) those which have not used it over this period, and (4) those which once used it but subsequently abolished it. They may also agree that if the average percentage increase in capital crimes per year in states that changed from no capital punishment to its use is less than the corresponding average in each of the other three categories, capital punishment is an effective deterrent; otherwise it is not.

If the opponents cannot agree on how to determine the match between actual and dissolving conditions, this disagreement should be made the subject of a debate that follows the procedure described here. Once this issue is resolved the original debate can continue.

> 4. Once agreement on how to establish the relevant conditions has been reached, the opponents should attempt to determine what these conditions actually are.

Presumably, the relevant facts will settle the issue. If such a determination is not possible or not feasible, the participants can proceed to the next step.

> 5. A "regret matrix" should be prepared in which the different positions being debated form the rows and the agreed-to justifying conditions form the columns.

Table 2.1 is such a matrix for the capital-punishment debate.

> 6. Now each of the opponents decides independently which of the two possible errors he believes to be the more serious. If the

Table 2.1.   Possible Errors on the Issue of Capital Punishment

	Justifying Conditions	
Positions	**Capital Punishment Deters Capital Crimes**	**Capital Punishment Does Not Deter Capital Crimes**
For capital punishment	X	Error 1
Against capital punishment	Error 2	X

opponents agree, they should accept the position that has the least serious error associated with it. If they do not agree, this becomes the issue they should take back to the first step.

The procedure described requires more control of discussion of an issue than opponents can usually provide by themselves. Therefore, a referee acceptable to both parties can be very helpful. The procedure is formal, but formalism often provides an effective way of settling disputes, as it does, for example, in courts of law.

There is no general agreement about whether there are some types of conflict that are incapable in principle of being resolved or dissolved. There is more general agreement, but less than unanimity, where practice, rather than principle, is involved. In practice most people believe that there are some conflicts that can be neither resolved nor dissolved. It seems obvious to some, for example, that if one party's ultimate objective is the destruction of another, resolution or dissolution is not possible in practice. Those who believe this would argue that conflicts such as those which arose out of Hitler's aspirations were conflicts that could not be resolved or dissolved. However, even in such cases there is room for doubt. Even homicidal maniacs have been talked out of intended aggressions.

The only thing that seems clear in this clouded area is that if a conflict is treated as though it cannot be resolved or dissolved, it will behave as though this were the case. The only way to prove that this is actually the case is to demonstrate that *every* way of trying to resolve or dissolve the conflict has failed or must fail. As far as I know, no one has ever done so for any conflict. Therefore, whenever circumstances permit, it seems desirable to make an effort at dissolution or resolution before resorting to force or submission.

SUMMARY

We began this discussion of objectives by distinguishing between those which are negative, directed at getting rid of something that is not wanted, and those which are positive, directed at getting something that is wanted. The type of formulation we use makes an important difference in our problem-solving efforts. With negative formulations we are more likely to overlook less-than-immediate consequences of our solutions. Therefore, by using negative formulations we tend to walk into the future facing the past.

Objectives (desired outcomes) are ends, and the courses of action we use to pursue them are means. However, means and ends are relative concepts. Means have both intrinsic and extrinsic value. Their intrinsic value lies in the satisfaction their use brings independent of what they bring about; their extrinsic value lies in their ability to bring about something else that we want. A persistent nonefficiency-based preference for a type of means is called a *trait,* and the collection of our traits constitutes our *style.* Our style is an essential part of our individuality. The formulation of objectives, therefore, should include specification of stylistic preferences.

Ends also have intrinsic and extrinsic value. Their intrinsic value lies in the satisfaction their attainment brings. Their extrinsic value lies in what they eventually lead to, their consequences, and therefore in the progress toward ultimate objectives, ideals, that their attainment brings about.

Effective problem formulation requires an awareness of possible consequences of actions beyond the outcome on which we focus. I argued that the focus should be on ideals and suggested that an explicit formulation of our relevant ideals enables those involved in a problem situation to make explicit their stylistic preferences as well.

Idealized design makes it possible for us to consider sets of interacting problems and to do so with a prospective rather than a retrospective orientation. This is an essential requirement of planning. Idealized design also facilitates the participation of all stakeholders, the generation of consensus among them, and the extension of their concepts of feasibility. Self-imposed constraints are relaxed in the idealization process. Joint consideration of solutions to interrelated problems tends to make solutions appear feasible that, if considered individually, appear to be infeasible.

Participative idealized design helps us to understand better our own objectives and those of the others involved in our problems. We frequently assume that others have objectives that they do not have in fact; we do so particularly when "we" and "they" are separated by a cultural gap. I suggested that we seek understanding of the objectives of others by assuming that their behavior is rational, no matter how irrational it may appear to us. The assumption of the irrationality of others prevents our understanding not only their behavior, but also our own. It conceals our own irrationality.

Differences of objectives among the stakeholders, or between the stakeholders and the decision maker, may breed conflict, a state in which the attainment of his objective by one party leads to the denial of the objectives of another party. We looked at three ways of dealing with conflict: solution, resolution, and dissolution.

To solve a conflict is to accept the situation and find the best one can do within it. To resolve a conflict is to accept the situation and find a distribution of gains and/or losses among opponents for which they are willing to settle. Resolutions are normally reached through some kind of negotiation. To dissolve a conflict is to change the situation in such a way as to remove the conflict. This may be done by changing either the environment or the opponents. The environment may be changed to separate the opponents, eliminate their interaction, remove a scarcity that is the source of their conflict, or change the objectives that are imposed on them from above.

In addition, a conflict may be dissolved by changing the opponents' choices of means or ends. Such changes may dissolve a conflict without loss to any of the parties involved, and possibly with gains to both. We considered the use of idealization and persuasion as ways of bringing about such changes. In this connection a formalized debating procedure that can change beliefs and values was presented.

There may be conflicts that cannot be resolved or dissolved without use of force, but no one has proved this to be the case. Therefore, efforts to dissolve or resolve conflicts should not be precluded a priori. To treat a conflict as though it were incapable of being dissolved or resolved is to engage in a self-fulfilling prophesy. This is a costly way of showing that one is "right," particularly when there is a good chance that one is actually wrong.

CHAPTER THREE

Controllable Variables

We can usually control a number of things in problematic situations, but many of them have no relevance to the problem in hand. For example, the fact that I can remove my coat has no relevance to my desire to get more light under which to read. On the other hand, in many problematic situations there are more relevant controllable variables than are considered. The relevant uncontrolled but controllable variables, if controlled, often make possible creative and effective solutions. Thus it is important to consciously take stock of, and deliberately determine, what is and what is not relevant.

We bring ready-made criteria of relevance to most problematic situations. Such criteria are derived from our education and previous experience with similar situations. It is not surprising, therefore, that economists tend to focus on economic variables in the same situation in which sociologists focus on sociological variables. Disciplinary education not only provides us with the ability to identify some controllable variables, but it also puts blinders on us that keep us from seeing others.

Whatever our criteria of relevance and however they are obtained, they often preclude our dealing with controllable variables that can be manipulated effectively. Consider, for example, the following story.

Table 3.1.   A FISHY STORY.

After World War II, as affluence increased in the British Isles, its inhabitants became less committed to discomfort: central heating and

Fable 3.1. A fishy story. Moral: One is often moved deeply by another's hunger.

refrigeration became increasingly common. With the increased use of refrigerators, freezing compartments were to be found in many homes. Therefore, the frozen-food business became more attractive.

A large food company decided to develop a line of frozen fish, an important source of protein in the British diet. The company was already a completely integrated fish producer and marketer. At one end, it had its own fishing fleet, and at the other it had its own chain of fish markets. It installed freezing and packaging equipment at its dockside plants to which its fleets brought their catches. Accompanied by a vigorous advertising campaign, it introduced frozen fish to the British consumer.

The initial trial rate was high, but sales dropped off sharply within a short time. It was clear that there were few second triers. The company put its market researchers to work to find out why. They learned from interviews of women who had tried their products that the taste of the fish was flat, not nearly as good as fresh fish.

After independently confirming the flatness by the use of taste panels, the company asked its food chemists to find the cause of the loss of flavor. The chemists put the blame on chemical changes that took place in dead fish, even though they were stored in ice on the trawlers. These changes, combined with the freezing process, resulted in the loss of flavor. The chemists recommended that the fish be frozen on board ship or that they be kept alive until they were brought to the freezing plant on shore.

The company then had its engineers carry out a comparison of the costs of these alternatives. They found it less expensive to keep the fish alive by converting the holds into pools into which the fish could be dumped from the nets in which they were caught. This was done. A new advertising campaign was launched. Again the initial number of trials was high, but the subsequent drop in sales was dramatic.

Another market survey was initiated. It revealed that the taste of the frozen fish was still flat. The food chemists were called in again. This time they found that the density of the fish in the holds was so great that they did not move about. This inactivity, the chemists said, produced the chemical changes responsible for the loss of flavor. They advised that the fish be kept active.

Engineers were again called in to find out how to make the fish move around in very densely occupied water. They set up tanks in a laboratory, filled them with water and fish, and experimented with various ways of disturbing the water to make the fish move about. Everything they tried failed. The fish remained inactive no matter how, or how much, the water was disturbed.

One day the laboratory was visited (for an unrelated reason) by an expert on the natural history of fish. He saw the tanks and asked what the engineers were trying to do to the fish in them. He listened to their explanation and patiently watched their efforts without comment. When the engineers had finished and he was about to leave he asked: "Why don't you try putting a predator in with them?"

They did and it worked: the fish moved to avoid being consumed before being frozen. Of course some failed and were lost, but this was a small price to pay for tasty frozen fish. The market for them subsequently thrived.

MORAL: One is often moved deeply by another's hunger.

Until recently I did not know whether this story was true. A short while ago, however, I used it in a lecture given in Sweden to a group of business executives. One of them told me that the use of predators in this way was commonplace on Norwegian trawlers.

The story, whether true or not, illustrates how simplifying a problem can make it more difficult to solve. The solution consisted of enlarging the system under study to include more of the larger system that contained it in reality.

We usually try to reduce complex situations to what appear to be one or more simple solvable problems. This is sometimes referred to as "cutting the problem down to size." In so doing we often reduce our chances of finding a creative solution to the original problem.

There is another important lesson to be learned from this last fable: the greater the variety of backgrounds of the people who examine a problematic situation, the greater the variety of variables that will be considered as susceptible to control. From this derives the widely observed problem-solving power of interdisciplinary teams.

The distinction between inter- and multidisciplinary teams is important. When a complex problem is divided into parts each of which is assigned to a different discipline for solution, the result is a multi-, not an interdisciplinary effort. In an interdisciplinary effort representatives of different disciplines work *together* in tackling the undivided problem however complex it is.

There is another fable, a classic of unknown origin, that has been repeated for more than a quarter of a century; it is too appropriate not to repeat at this point.

Fable 3.2.   AN UPS-AND-DOWNS STORY.

The manager of a large office building had been receiving an increasing number of complaints about the building's elevator service, particularly during rush hours. When several of his larger tenants threatened to move out unless this service was improved, the manager decided to look into the problem.

He called on a group of consulting engineers who specialized in the design of elevator systems. After examining the situation, they identified three possible courses of action: (1) add elevators, (2) replace some or all of the existing elevators with faster ones, or (3) add a central computerized control system so that the elevators could be "routed" to yield faster service.

The engineers then conducted cost-benefit analyses of these alternatives. They found that only adding or replacing elevators could yield a large enough improvement of service, but the cost of doing either was not justified by the earnings of the building. In effect, none of the alternatives was acceptable. They left the manager with this dilemma.

The manager then did what a manager seldom does when he is anything less than desperate: he consulted his subordinates. He called a meeting of his staff and presented the problem to them in the format of what he called a "brain-storming" session. Many suggestions were made, but each was demolished. The discussion slowed down. During a lull the new young assistant in the personnel department, who had been quiet up to this point, timidly made a suggestion. It was immediately embraced by everyone present. A few weeks later, after a relatively small expenditure, the problem had disappeared.

Full-length mirrors had been installed on all the walls of the elevator lobbies on each floor.

The young personnel psychologist had reasoned that the complaints originated from the boredom of waiting for elevators. The actual waiting time was quite small, but it *seemed* long because of the lack of anything to do while waiting. He gave people something to do: look at themselves and others (particularly of the opposite sex) without appearing to do so. This kept them pleasantly occupied.

> **MORAL: With reflection it becomes apparent that there is more than one way to look at a problem.**

Our natural inclination is to try to find the cause of the deficiency that gives rise to a problem and to remove or suppress it. We did this unsuccessfully in the case of Prohibition and we are doing it again with respect to the misuse of narcotics. Unfortunately, even if we get rid of what we do not want, we do not necessarily obtain what we do want. When I change a television channel to remove a distasteful program, I seldom get one that is satisfactory. Health is more than the absence of disease, even though many doctors act as though they are equivalent. Efforts to remove deficiencies are not without success, but there is an alternative approach to problem solving that should also be considered because it is often more effective: adding something to, rather than subtracting something from, a problematic situation to convert a malefactor into a benefactor. Consider, for example, this fable.

Fable 3.3. ON DRIVING A HARD BARGAIN.

An automobile insurance company that is a subsidiary of an automobile manufacturing company asked Aesop for assistance because it was not operating profitably. Most of the cars it insured were made by the parent company and sold new by dealers who also sold the insurance. Because of the nature of the cars made by the parent company, many of them were bought by young unmarried males who are the most accident-prone drivers on the road. Therefore, the company blamed its failure to make money on "adverse selection" of insurees. It wanted to determine how to insure fewer high-risk drivers and more who were low risks.

This could hardly be done without changing the styling of the cars made by the parent company to attract purchases by more conservative drivers. The insurance company could, of course, have refused to insure young unmarried males, but if it did so it would have run the risk of reducing sales of the cars made by its parent company.

Aesop felt that the problem had been incorrectly formulated; thus he directed his efforts at finding out how to make young unmarried males better drivers. His research into the causes of accidents revealed, among other things, that (1) drivers of vehicles who can see *over* vehicles in front of them respond to what is happening further in front of them and hence are less likely to become involved in accidents; and (2) drivers of vehicles whose operators or owners can easily be identified, such as trucks and busses, are less accident prone because their bad driving is often reported by others to the owners or police.

These observations led Aesop to two recommendations. First, he suggested that the parent company equip automobiles with retractable periscopes mounted near the rear-view mirror so that drivers of low vehicles could look over those in front of them. Second, he suggested that for six months after he caused an accident, an insuree, if he wanted to continue being insured, would have to mount on any vehicle he drove a plate that identified him and therefore indicated that he had recently been the cause of an accident. Aesop argued that this would make other drivers behave more defensively when near him, and it would make him drive more self-consciously and cautiously.

> **MORAL: Looking over something may not be an oversight.**

The recommendations made by Aesop were rejected as "unrealistic." Subsequently, however, taxis in a foreign city were experimentally equipped with periscopes, with a significant reduction of accidents. Another foreign city has experimented with special license plates on cars driven by those responsible for a recent accident. It too reported a reduction of accidents. England has used a variation of this idea by requiring all learners to mount a large plate with an "L" on it on any vehicle they drive.

If half the attention given to making automobiles safer in the event of an accident were given to designing them so they would be less likely to be involved in accidents, we might be better off. I am reminded of an outrageous but wonderful suggestion made by my friend Stafford Beer, the eminent British cybernetician: that instead of inserting an inflatable balloon between driver and dashboard in the event of an accident, spikes should be placed on the dashboard facing the driver. This would ensure his involvement in fewer accidents.

Perhaps more acceptable is a device that determines the distance to the vehicle in front of the one in which it is installed. It also calculates the maximum safe speed in light of this distance and prevents the vehicle from exceeding it.

What is added to a situation to convert something that is destructive into something that is constructive may not be a thing but *temptation,* as the next two fables illustrate.

Fable 3.4.   TIME ON THEIR HANDS.

A company that produced small precision-made parts employed a large number of women as inspectors of its finished products. The women were paid a flat daily rate that was independent of their output. Their productivity was decreasing significantly, and the number of incorrectly accepted and rejected items was increasing at the same time. Hopeful of increasing productivity and reducing errors, the plant manager proposed a piece-rate compensation plan that would make it possible for the women to earn significantly more money if their output increased to a previously attained level. If they maintained their then-current level, however, they would earn less. The women rejected the proposal summarily.

The manager was surprised by this response and was left without an alternative. He called for help from an externally based research group that was working on another unrelated problem in his plant.

The researchers found that most of the women were married and their husbands were employed and earned enough money to provide their families with necessities. The women were working to increase the amount of money available for discretionary goods and services, things they wanted but did not really need. The women did not want to earn as much as their husbands because they believed this would threaten their husbands' self-image as breadwinners. (This was before the feminist movement got under way.) Thus they were not anxious to earn more than they were alredy earning. Furthermore, working carelessly at a leisurely pace enabled the women to socialize with co-workers while doing their jobs, thereby getting some relief from their dull and repetitive task.

More important, the researchers discovered that most of the women had children in school and felt very guilty about not being at home to receive their children when they returned from school. The children either had to take care of themselves, which was a cause of anxiety for their mothers, or they were cared for by others on whom the mothers felt they were imposing. In either case the women held the company responsible for creating this uncomfortable and guilt-ridden situation.

When the researchers learned this, they designed a new incentive system. A "fair day's work"—the number of items correctly inspected—was specified. It was set at the highest level of output the women had previously attained. However, the women were permitted to leave work and return home whenever they finished the specified output, or they could continue on a piece-rate basis for as much additional time as they desired and production requirements permitted. The women accepted this proposal enthusiastically. Their inspection rate more than doubled, and they were out of the plant in plenty of time to meet their children returning from school. Errors decreased and satisfaction increased.

MORAL: Nothing consumes time like nothing.

A manager in one of the District Banks of the Federal Reserve System who heard me tell this story offered a similar arrangement to his male coin counters. They also accepted enthusiastically, but for different reasons: it enabled them to take on a second job and still have some time for leisure.

In some situations it is desirable, of course, to remove temptation, but this can seldom be done effectively without adding something to take its place, as the next fable shows.

Fable 3.5.   IT TAKES A THIEF . . .

The leaders of a self-development group from an urban "Black ghetto" came to Aesop to seek help with a neighborhood problem. They were concerned about thefts from, robberies of, and vandalism to retail stores in the neighborhood. These had increased so much that insurance companies refused to insure retailers against such aggression. As a result, the retailers were leaving the area in increasing numbers and were not being replaced. The neighborhood already suffered from grossly inadequate shopping facilities.

A discussion of the problem revealed that most of the thefts, holdups, and damage was caused by members of youthful gangs that flourished in the neighborhood. Police coverage of the area was not sufficient to protect the merchants, and efforts by the merchants to increase it had failed.

Rather than try to protect the merchants from the gangs or to remove the culprits, Aesop sought to convert them into a constructive force. He found a way to do so.

The community leaders asked the merchants to employ gang members as helpers. A number agreed to do so. Aggression against merchants stopped. Word got around, and other merchants followed suit. The emigration of merchants stopped, and they no longer required insurance.

MORAL: Care is often the most effective cure.

In some situations incentives may already be operating, but they may be responsible for the very behavior that causes a problem. Incentives are tricky things. They are not always deliberate or conspicuous; hence we are frequently unaware of them even when we are influenced by them. When we are aware of incentives, we often assume that they have an effect other than that which they actually have. Again some examples.

Fable 3.6.   FOR WHOM THE BRIDGE TOLLS.

The Port Authority of a major American city controls, among other things, all bridges and tunnels into its metropolitan area. Like most such authorities it offers reduced rates to heavy users of the facilities. This, of course, encourages commutation by automobile into the city. It also contributes significantly to traffic congestion in the city. The Port Authority was not inclined to discourage commuters by raising tolls because its income depended on them, yet it was under pressure from the city's traffic department to help reduce congestion. Aesop was consulted.

Studies had shown that most cars coming into the city had only one or two persons in them. The average was well below two. Therefore, there were more empty than filled seats in these cars. There was no incentive for a driver to fill his car with passengers by car pooling because tolls were independent of occupancy. Aesop proposed charging for the number of empty seats in an automobile, with no charge for cars that were filled. The cost per empty seat could then be set to produce as much income as was desired and could be adjusted to changing usage as required. Aesop argued that such a toll system would encourage both car pooling and the use of smaller automobiles, both of which would reduce traffic in the city.

> **MORAL: One should not be charged for full-filling activity.**

Aesop's proposal was rejected because it was believed to be politically infeasible and because toll collection would be too complicated. (This despite the fact that some bridges, tunnels, and ferries charge for the number of seats filled in a car.) Subsequently, however, a variant of Aesop's proposal was introduced successfully on the Bay Bridge in the San Francisco area. There, cars with more than a specified number of passengers can use the bridge at no cost and have the use of reserved express lanes at peak hours.

Fable 3.7.   THE TRUCK THAT RUNNETH OVER.

One of the operating companies of the Bell System asked Aesop to try to reduce the amount of stock carried in trucks driven by service men who called on subscribers to repair, replace, install, or remove telephones. In a normal day a serviceman made only a relatively small number of calls. Nevertheless, because he did not know what parts he would require and because his compensation was based on the number of calls he completed per day, he filled his truck with every part he could get into it.

Aesop designed a new compensation system to replace the old one. He made a repairman's compensation a function of both the number of calls he completed *and* the value of the stock he carried in his truck; the larger the stock, the less the compensation. This yielded very large reductions of in-transit inventories, with only a very small reduction in the average number of calls completed per day.

> **MORAL: Even a telephone repairman can get a wrong number.**

The system involved in each of the previous two fables provided incentives that produced the behavior that caused the problem. Of course they were not intended to do so. They were designed to serve one objective in situations in which more than one objective was operating. An incentive that serves one objective may well serve another very badly.

The design of an effective incentive system clearly requires understanding the objectives of those to be "incented." This is obvious. What is not so obvious is that design of an effective incentive system also requires the designer to have a clear understanding of his own objectives, as the next fable shows.

Fable 3.8.   STOP-OR-GO DRIVING.

At approximately the same time two very different schemes were developed to reduce automotive congestion in New York City and London. The New York proposal consisted of placing electronic sensing devices along streets in the city. These devices were to read magnetized numbers placed on the sides of automobiles and transmit them to a central computer that would collect and use them to prepare charges to car owners for the use of city streets. It was intended that the amount billed per reading would depend on the time at which the reading was made—the day of the week and the time of day. Charges would be greatest when congestion was greatest. It was hoped that in this way the use of automobiles during peak hours would be discouraged. Needless to say, the sensing-communication-computing system required by this design was both very complex and very costly.

The scheme developed for London was based on installing meters in each car so that its mileage in the city could be determined periodically, as, for example, at car-inspection time or when leaving the city. Charges would be made on a mileage basis. This was the simpler of the two schemes but its rate structure was not adaptive to traffic conditions as was the scheme developed for New York.

Aesop was called on to evaluate these alternatives and select the better of the two. He observed that both schemes charged automobiles for "going." Congestion, however, is not measured by how much cars go; rather it is measured by how much they stop. Therefore, Aesop argued, what is needed is a disincentive to stopping, not going. This, he showed, could be accomplished by the use of a very simple metering device that would count the number of stops a car made and charge a fixed rate per stop. Such a system would automatically take account of traffic conditions. If a trip were taken at peak hours on a work day, its cost would be high because of the number of stops required. The same trip taken at off hours would be much less expensive. Furthermore, such a scheme would encourage the use of less-traveled routes, and it would encourage drivers to try to avoid stopping at lights by slowing down when approaching one that is red. This would increase through-put at lights where start-up time of vehicles at rest currently consumes much of the "go time."

**MORAL: It may be better to think without stopping
than to stop and think.**

It is easy to fall into the trap into which the designers of the disincentive system involved in the last fable fell. Subtlety and sophistication in incentives are generally not as effective as simplicity and directness. The intentions of an incentive system should be obvious to those who are supposed to be affected by them.

It is important to get one's objectives straight not only before designing an incentive system, but also before designing any system that might be perceived by others as providing an incentive, however unintended. For example, consider the way property is taxed in most of the United States. Such taxes are generally proportional to the assessed value of the property. Therefore, they provide an incentive that encourages allowing property to deteriorate. That such taxes operate in this way is apparent in urban ghettos. No wonder we have so much rapidly deteriorating housing in most American cities.

If, in addition to taxing the value of property, we also taxed the *reduction of its value over time*, we would provide an incentive for its maintenance and improvement. Some countries offer tax exemptions for the maintenance and improvement of residential property, much as we provide them for business properties.

What is wrong in a problematic situation is often far from apparent, however apparent it may be that something is wrong. For example, we may know that we are ill without knowing the cause of our illness. Diagnosis then becomes a critical phase of problem solving. The use of an effective cure for an ailment that we do not have may not only fail to cure us, it may make us even more seriously ill.

Where there are a number of cases of similar failures the causes of which are not known, a suggestion made many years ago by the British philosopher John Stuart Mill may serve well: *look for something that is common to each failure and that is never present when there is a success.* Consider the next example.

Fable 3.9.   IT MAY HURT TO BEND A LITTLE.

In a conversation held in the mid-fifties with a friend who was a manager in a large company that manufactured major household appliances, Aesop said that in the long run consumers were seldom irrational but producers of consumer goods often were. The manager challenged this statement and offered what he thought were some counterexamples.

He said that since the electric refrigerator had been put on the market there had been a number of successful and unsuccessful introductions of appliances that could not be explained by consumer rationality. Rather, he argued, they demonstrated the irrationality of consumers. Then he gave examples of what he maintained were an irrational failure and an irrational success.

Market surveys, he said, had indicated that dish washing was considered by housewives to be the most unpleasant household task. Yet his company had recently introduced an automatic dishwasher that had been poorly received by consumers. On the other hand, he pointed out, the counter-top cooking range and built-in oven and broiler were very successful even though they did nothing not done by the "old-fashioned" range, and together they were more expensive than the old range. How, he asked, could Aesop explain these on the basis of consumer rationality?

Aesop said that answers to such questions were not easy to come by. They usually required extended research. The manager was skeptical about the value of such research but indicated a willingness to take a "quick-and-dirty" look at the problem. Aesop suggested that he place one of each successful appliance that his company had introduced on one side of a large showroom at the plant, and one of each unsuccessful appliance on the other side. Aesop also asked that the manager not enter the showroom until they could do so together. The manager agreed.

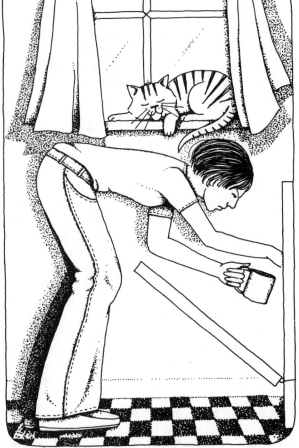

Fable 3.9. It may hurt to bend a little. Moral: It is easy to blame others for our own mistakes, but it is hard to correct them by doing so.

A short time later the manager called Aesop and said that the room was ready. They met with mock ceremony and entered the room. Neither said a word; they just looked. Within a minute or so the manager admitted that Aesop's assertion about consumer rationality held.

What they had observed was that every one of the successful appliances could be used without bending or climbing, whereas every one of the unsuccessful ones required bending or climbing. The dishwasher, at that time, required loading by putting dishes into it from the front; it could not be loaded without squatting. On the other hand, the built-in oven could be used without bending, whereas the one in the old-fashioned range could not.

Before Aesop and the manager left the room, the manager initiated work on modifying both appliances. First, he asked that a dishwasher be designed with pull-out drawers so that it could be loaded without squatting and, second, that a cooking range be designed with the oven and broiler above, not below, the cooking unit, using the vacated space below the burners for storage.

> **MORAL: It is easy to blame others for our own
> mistakes, but it is hard to correct them
> by doing so.**

Despite this fable, consumers are not always rational, but in my experience I have found them to be so more often than producers. Consumers have more chances to learn by trial and error than producers. Many producers devote their marketing efforts, particularly advertising, to trying to convince consumers that significant product differences exist where they do not. The curious thing is that such efforts succeed in convincing the producer more often than the consumer. Producers often come to believe the deceptions they pay to propogate.

Gasoline is a case in point. It is apparent that if we filled identical makes and models of automobile with different brands of the same grade of gasoline, not even the presidents of oil companies could identify the brands by their performances. Yet their advertising tries to convince consumers that there are significant performance differences between brands.

Many years ago some of my colleagues conducted research for an oil company to determine what led consumers to the selection of the service station they normally used. They found that one variable, *not* brand, had a greater effect than all the other variables put together. Furthermore, this variable made it clear that consumers were behaving rationally, given no difference in brands. This variable and its discovery are revealed in Fable 5.4.

Where there are no significant differences between alternatives offered by producers, it is more effective in general to invest in creating such differences than to try to convince others that they exist where they do not. Here is a case in point.

Fable 3.10.   THE INSIDE-OUT PROBLEM.

Another manager of a major appliance manufacturing company complained that it was becoming increasingly difficult to maintain, let alone increase, his company's share of the refrigerator market, because there were no significant differences between different makes. Aesop suggested that he direct research at creating such differences. The manager said that he had already done so without success. A discussion of the nature of these efforts revealed that none of them had involved a study of the consumers' use of refrigerators. Aesop proposed a small study of such use on the grounds that it might reveal how a refrigerator could be significantly improved *from the consumers' point of view.* The manager agreed.

Aesop found that the most common reason for opening a refrigerator was to get ice or cold water. Therefore, he suggested designing a refrigerator that dispensed ice cubes and cold water without opening its door, that is, by means of a dispenser built into the door. It was many years before this suggestion was taken seriously, but when it was it was very successful.

MORAL: Many a hot idea gets a cold shoulder.

We tend to accept, and lose awareness of, persistent inconveniences, particularly minor ones. Identifying and eliminating them can lead to improvements that are significant because a persistent minor inconvenience may be more annoying than an occasional major one.

There are many examples of successes obtained by improving what we take for granted. A very familiar one was the placing the abrasive for striking a paper match on the back of the package rather than the front. This removed the necessity for closing the book before striking.

Consider a minor but persistent inconvenience to heavy travellers. They must either reset their watches whenever they go from one time zone to another, or they must adjust their readings of their unreset watches. One watch producer has made the outer ring of a wrist watch on which the hours are marked rotatable so that the watch can be reset without resetting its hands. The disadvantage of this is that the position of the hours changes: twelve o'clock, for example, is no longer at the top of the watch. This creates its own annoyance and inconvenience.

If the outer ring with the hour markings on it were left stationary, but the watch itself, including its arms, could be rotated within the ring, all the inconvenience would be removed. No resetting of the hands would be required, and the watch would always have the same orientation.

To this point we have considered problem situations that are relatively static, ones in which the essential features are not changing rapidly. However, change itself is becoming a source of problems. Charles Snow, Geoffrey Vickers, Peter Drucker, Alvin Toffler, Donald Schon, and many others have argued that the accelerating rate of technological and social change is now the source of our major societal and organizational difficulties. Many of these changes are occurring more rapidly than we adapt to them, hence the dislocations and lags from which we suffer.

Although a rapid rate of change creates many current problems, it also creates many opportunities. These can be anticipated by the use of what I call "reference projections." These are extrapolations from the past into the future under an assumption we know to be false: that things will continue to be done and to happen much as they have in the past, that is, without significant interventions by decision makers or the environment. Because reference projections are based on a false assumption, they do not yield predictions of things to come; they do predict what will not or is *not* likely to happen. They do this by showing how a system would break down if it were to continue to operate in the future as it has in the past. Such breakdowns are not likely to occur because there will be interventions. By revealing these points of future breakdown *now*, effective interventions can be planned before a future crisis forces a rapid and less effective intervention.

For example, in a projection of the paper work performed by the Federal Reserve Bank of Cleveland, it was found that the amount of space required to do the amount of work projected to the year 2000 would exceed the amount of commercial space available in Cleveland at that time. This "revelation" helped spur the development of an Electronic Funds Transfer System which would greatly reduce the space requirement and has a number of other advantages as well.

In a projection of the number of automobiles in the United States in the year 2000, it was found that there would not be enough surface in metropolitan areas on which to place them. Such a projection, of course, is not a forecast of what will happen but, as noted, of what will not. What will happen depends on decisions to be made between now and then. The recognition of a future crisis can induce us to think now about alternative courses of action, creative ones that might avert the crisis. These often involve the fundamental redesign of the system involved, as is the case involving the automobile that is presented in Chapter 7.

Reference projections are not so much a way of finding solutions to problems as they are a way of identifying the problems that ought to be solved. Recall that formulating the right problem is at least as important as getting the right solution. Such projections also reveal what controllable aspects of a system or a situation require change.

There is one aspect of reference projections that requires caution:

the changing meaning of concepts. For example, in the 1950s a projection was made that showed that everyone in the United States would soon be a scientist if current trends continued. On the face of it this projection seemed silly, but it was not. Suppose that at the time of Newton a similar projection had been made of the number of mathematicians in England today. In all likelihood it would have shown that all Englishmen would be mathematicians. In a sense this would have been close to correct. Many, if not most, people in England today know as much mathematics as Newton did (without necessarily understanding it as he did), but those now called mathematicians know a great deal more. *The requirements for being a mathematician have also changed.*

Therefore, in reference projecting one should be careful to determine whether the meaning of the units being projected are subject to change over the period covered.

To this point we have dealt only with constraints implicitly. Now let us consider them explicity—first, those self-imposed constraints of which we are not aware.

As previously mentioned, our selection of the variables to manipulate in any given situation is conditioned by our previous experience and our education. As a result we unconsciously preclude from consideration certain types of controllable variables and confine our attention to certain traditional ones. Consider the next example.

Table 3.11. BANKING IN THE NUDE.

Over time several thefts of money and other valuables had been committed by employees of a large financial institution despite an extensive security system. For example, there were check-in and check-out points to cover the entry and exit of everyone, numerous armed guards posted throughout the facility, closed-circuit television surveillance of all work areas, multiple doors to valuables each locked with keys held by separate guards, and so on. The cost of such a system was very large, yet it was "defeated" with regularity.

The thefts were almost always committed by small teams of employees because the tasks in the institution were so divided, and so many internal checks were made that it was almost impossible for a single individual to cover a theft long enough to get out of the facilities or, if he did, to avoid rapid identification.

Research was initiated to find a way of tightening the institution's security. The alternatives considered were the obvious ones. These included such things as the number, location, and rotation of guards, more extensive use of electronic detection devices, and the rotation of work assignments at random within the bank at frequent enough intervals to make the formulation of criminal coalitions less likely.

Aesop was asked to review this project. After the presentation, he asked how the thieves removed what they stole from the bank. He was told that the stolen valuables were usually concealed on the person or in his or her personal effects. Bills of large denomination, for example, do not require much space. Why, Aesop asked, is there not a more thorough search at the point of exit? He was told that, because of the number of employees, this would be very time consuming and would not necessarily be effective unless a person was examined in the nude. Aesop asked why they did not work in the nude. Everyone laughed, but Aesop continued: "I know this is not feasible, but it suggests that all employees be required to wear a uniform changed into and out of at work. This could make inspection in the nude 'natural' and unobtrusive." Aesop went on to explain that uniforms could be designed to facilitate work, save on personal clothing, and be attractive.

The solution suggested by Aesop was not accepted. Instead, surveillance was significantly increased. The thefts continued.

MORAL: Bare facts cannot be concealed.

I cannot help but recall the old story of the worker at a large factory who left work each night pushing a wheelbarrow full of waste. The guard at the gate noted this repeated event and even inspected the waste but could find nothing of value in it. It was only much later that he discovered that the worker had been stealing wheelbarrows.

Now consider a case in which the suggestion that something commonplace and traditional not be taken for granted was taken seriously.

Fable 3.12.   MAKING PAPER WORK.

The production manager of a large paper company for which Aesop had previously done research asked him for assistance in a production-scheduling problem. The manager explained that he had a large number of different papers to produce over a relatively small number of production lines. Therefore, he frequently had to change production lines from making one product to another. Because of an increasing number of orders for low-volume products, the number of change-overs (setups) on his production lines and the time they consumed were increasing. Therefore, the amount of time spent in production was decreasing, and the overheaded unit cost of production was increasing. The manager wanted to find a way of scheduling production so that the total setup time was minimized.

Aesop pointed out that a mathematical procedure for solving this type of problem was available. He suggested that it be applied retrospectively for the last five years assuming that a perfect forecast of sales had been available. This, he said, would enable him to determine the maximum possible improvement. If this were not significantly large, there would be no point in going ahead along this line. If it were large enough, a second run could be made using forecasts with the same accuracy as those currently in use. The manager agreed.

Aesop's calculations revealed that with a perfect forecast a substantial reduction in production costs could be obtained, but he also found that with the quality of forecasting available the improvement that could be obtained hardly justified the effort. This appeared to reduce the problem to one of improving forecasting of future demand.

While collecting data to begin work on the forecasting problem, Aesop learned that about ten percent of the products accounted for about ninety percent of the sales and a still higher percentage of corporate profits. Many of the low-volume products were sold at a loss.

These findings diverted Aesop from his forecasting effort. He prepared a list of all the company's products from the most to the least profitable. This took some time, but once it was completed he turned to this question: If the company starts to drop products from its product line beginning with the least profitable and working its way up the list, how many products would the company have to drop before—with the scheduling and forecasting procedure then in use—it could obtain a reduction in production cost equal to the theoretical maximum revealed by his previous analysis?

The answer surprised Aesop: less than five percent, all of which were unprofitable.

Aesop then suggested to the production manager that this was a more promising approach to his problem than the one he had previously taken. The manager agreed but said that dropping products from the product line was out of his control. This was the responsibility of the vice president of marketing. Previous discussions with this vice president on dropping products, the production manager said, had been to no avail. Aesop asked if he could talk to the vice president. The production manager reluctantly agreed, saying that he thought it would be a waste of time.

When Aesop met with the vice president of marketing, he reviewed his analyses and the conclusion he had drawn from them. The vice president was not surprised by these results. He asked Aesop if he had considered who were the purchasers of the unprofitable products. Aesop admitted that he had not. Well, the vice president said, if Aesop had done so he would have found these purchasers to be the major consumers of the company's profitable products. He added that he could not afford to run the risk of losing these customers by discontinuing the unprofitable products. Aesop asked how he knew that any risk was involved. The vice president admitted that he had no such knowledge, but he was unwilling to drop products to find out. Aesop asked if he would consider dropping products if a riskless way of doing so could be found. The vice president said he would be willing to do so but he did not think there was any such way. Aesop asked for some time to think it over; he was down but not yet out.

In thinking about the problem Aesop recalled that the company's salesmen were paid a fixed salary plus a commission based on the dollar value of their sales. This meant they earned as much for selling a dollar's worth of unprofitable products as for selling the same amount of profitable products. Because the unprofitable products were "underpriced" and therefore a good buy, Aesop suspected that they received a disproportional amount of the salesmen's attention. (Salesmen had no information about each product's profitability.) This led Aesop to consider a compensation plan for salesmen with these characteristics:

1. It would pay a commission proportional to the profitability of a sale and pay no commission for unprofitable sales.

2. The commission rates would be set so that if they had been in effect for the last five years and this had had no effect on what the salesmen had sold, their annual earnings would have been the same. On the other hand, if they had sold more of the profitable products and less of the unprofitable ones, they would have earned more.

After developing such a compensation system, Aesop returned to the vice president of marketing. He pointed out that if the vice president's suspicion about customer behavior was correct, the salesmen would either know this or learn it very quickly. Therefore, there would be little or no risk in adopting the compensation system. If, however, by some remote chance the vice president were wrong, he would find this out by the use of the system, and both the company and salesmen would benefit, not to mention the vice president. Furthermore, production costs would decrease, and the company's products could then be priced more attractively.

The vice president agreed to a trial of Aesop's plan in one marketing area. The results exceeded even Aesop's expectations. Sales of profitable products increased substantially, and a large portion of the unprofitable products were not sold at all. The salesmen earned more, company profits increased, and the production problem dissolved. The compensation system was then extended to cover all salesmen and markets.

MORAL: That which is lost may not be found where the loss is found.

The profit-based incentive system revealed that a constraint that was apparently imposed by customers was actually imposed by the marketing manager.

There is an old story the moral of which is not unrelated to that of the previous fable. A drunk was on his hands and knees crawling about under a street light on a dark night, obviously looking for something. A passerby stopped to ask him what he was looking for. He said he was looking for his keys. After a moment he added that he had lost them back in a nearby alley. The passerby asked him why, then, was he looking for them where he was. He answered, "Because it's light here."

Our conceptions of what can be done in problematic situations are often limited by constraints attributed to technology. We frequently forget or overlook the fact that technology and its use are controllable. What appears to be a technological constraint to one person may not appear so to another.

I have heard, for example, that the makers of Scotch Tape did not envision most of the uses to which their product was put. Inventive consumers discovered these uses, but the company was resourceful enough to adapt their product to these uses.

Problems are often caused by the misuse or abuse of technology. We often try to solve problems by prohibiting or suppressing such misuse or abuse. The intended results are often more easily obtained by minor modifications in the technology involved. For example, consider photocopying equipment.

Anyone who has access to such equipment can reproduce copyrighted material without paying the royalties to which the copyright holder is legally entitled. Nevertheless such practice is common. It is virtually impossible to enforce a law that prohibits this practice or to collect royalties from those who engage in it.

The issue raised by current copying practices are being hotly debated in Congress and among authors, publishers, librarians, educators, and students, all of whom are significantly affected by the issue. More restrictive laws are not likely to be enforceable as long as photocopying machines can be used in private. At best such laws can only be enforced in libraries that are open to the public and at commercial reproduction services, but this would be costly and would cover only a small portion of current infractions.

Publishers have also sought a technological solution, for example, an ink that could not be copied by the infernal machines. However, no one has been able to find a practical way of preventing the abuse.

Recently a research group at my university came up with a different approach. It has yet to be developed in detail, but it opens a new set of alternative solutions.

Photocopying machines are of two types: machines that can copy pages of bound volumes and ones that cannot. To use the latter, individual pages are usually fed through rollers. The former usually involves placing the page to be copied, bound or unbound, face down on a transparent plate. The roller-fed machine cannot be used to copy pages in a bound document. Unbinding the document is both costly and time consuming.

Therefore, the research group proposed a tax per copy made on non-roller-fed machines, with these exceptions: libraries and commercial reproduction services would collect royalties for copies of copyrighted material made on their machines and forward them to the appropriate places. This much could be enforced.

The tax could be based on periodic readings of the meters on non-single-sheet machines. Most such machines are currently rented and charged for a per-copy basis. The number of copies is determined by reading a meter on the machine. Therefore, the tax could be collected by the machine supplier and forwarded to the government. Once the cost of collection and administration of the tax were deducted from receipts, the remainder could be divided among publishers proportionally to the dollar value of their sales as reported on their tax forms. The payments could be made in the form of corporate tax allowances.

The proposed procedure would encourage the use of roller-fed copiers for normal use because no tax would be involved. It would also pressure publishers to price their products competitively with "reproduction-plus-tax" costs and therefore to seek new technology that would reduce the cost of printing. Such pressures might even result in publishers using photocopying equipment for this purpose. For example, document production might eventually be decentralized and copies be made to order from a master copy supplied by the publisher. This would remove one of the largest problems currently facing publishers: deciding how many copies of a document to make per printing.

In most attempts to solve the illicit reproduction of copyrighted material, consideration has not been given to the use of a tax or the difference between types of copying machines. Once these are raised to consciousness, a large number of possibilities is opened for consideration.

Sometimes the technology required to solve a problem lies in front of our noses without our being aware of it. We miss it because of our preconception of where technology is to be found: among those who are technologically educated. This is not always the case. Here are two examples.

Fable 3.13.   THE SMART JACKASS.

A team of faculty members and students from the National Autonomous University of Mexico were working with a group of "backward" farmers in a very underdeveloped part of Mexico. They were trying to encourage these "campesinos" to improve themselves and their lot. The academics made themselves available as resources to be used by the campesinos as they saw fit.

The campesinos were very responsive and decided to try to irrigate their fields by digging a large ditch from a water source to the fields and smaller ditches to distribute the water over the fields. To do this they needed to determine level paths over their hilly fields. The academics said they could help by getting some surveying equipment from the university.

The campesinos told them this would not be necessary. They told the academics that if a burro is held at one point and something he wants and can see is placed at another point, if left free he will take a level path from origin to destination. The academics were skeptical and got their equipment anyhow. They tested the burro and found it to be as good as they were.

> **MORAL: The easiest way to do something is often learned the hard way.**

The more pride one takes in what one knows, the harder it is to learn from others, particularly unlikely others, as the next fable shows.

Fable 3.14.   SPIT IS A NATURAL RESOURCE.

Several highly trained engineers were trying to instrument an old steel-making furnace to determine the temperature of the steel in the center

Fable 3.13. The smart jackass. Moral: The easiest way to do something is often learned the hard way.

of the furnace. They were doing this on the shop floor while the old operator of the furnace, who had received no explanation of their activity, stood watching them. After several unsuccessful tries, the overheated and frustrated technicians took a break.

The old man then asked them what they were trying to do. They indulged him and explained. He diffidently said that he could tell them how to do it without instruments. They indulged him again and asked how.

The old man, who was chewing tobacco, expectorated, placing a large wad of spittle onto the side of the furnace and then consulted his wrist watch. In a few seconds he "announced" the temperature. When asked for an explanation, he said his predecessor had taught him that by timing the evaporation of spittle as he had done and multiplying it by a number he had been given, he would get the temperature at the center of the furnace. The technicians smiled indulgently.

Days later when they had found a way to instrument the furnace, they decided to have fun with the old man and test him. They did so much to their regret. He was right.

MORAL: There may be more technology in an old hand than in a new mind.

These examples show that constraints imposed on *where* we look for solutions often preclude creative and effective solutions to problems. Location is not the only spatial property that constrains our problem-solving efforts; dimensionality is another.

The term "organizational structure" immediately conjures up an image of a two-dimensional tree-like diagram consisting of boxes and lines. The boxes designate jobs to be done, areas of responsibility, and thus represent how the labor of the organization is divided. Altitude and lines represent the flow of authority; that is, the occupant of a box has direct authority over the occupant of a lower box connected to the first by a solid line. The relationships considered are restricted to two dimensions: up and down and across, because we operate with the constraining assumption that an organization's structure must be representable in a two-dimensional chart that can be drawn on a flat surface.

There is nothing in the meaning of organizational structure that constrains us in this way. Furthermore, these constraints have consequences in the organizations we form that are often serious and costly. I mention only three. First, the organizations they yield often breed competition rather than cooperation among the parts. I have heard it said that there is more competition within organizations than between them, and the internal type is much less ethical. Second, the conventional way of representing organizations makes the operational definition of unit objectives and the measurement of related performance very difficult because of the great interdependence of units so conceived. Third, it tends to encourage organizations that resist change, particularly of structure; hence they move toward nonadaptive bureaucracy. Most such organizations learn very slowly if they learn at all.

Such deficiencies can and have been overcome by designing "multidimensional" organizations. One such design is developed in detail in Chapter 8.

The conventional way of representing and thinking about organizational structure leads to a dilemma that has become increasingly prominent as the movement toward participative democracy in organizations has gained momentum. The dilemma appears to arise out of two conflicting requirements.

First, there is the *hierarchical* requirement. Complex tasks must be divided into parts that can be performed by individuals or groups. These individuals or groups must be coordinated if the larger task is to be completed successfully. If there are a large number of coordinators, they require coordination, and so on. Out of this hierarchy arise levels of authority, which are essential for the effective organization of a large number of interdependent tasks.

Second, there is the *democratic* requirement. In a democracy no individual may be subjected to the control of another who is not subject to control by those over whom he has some control. In government, for example, all officials are subject to "the will of the governed."

How can an industrial organization, or a hospital or a university, be structured hierarchically and be democratic at the same time? Most people believe these two organizational principles to be antithetical and therefore feel forced to select one or the other. As a result, our democratic societies are thickly populated with autocratic organizations.

We need not sacrifice hierarchy or democracy if we remove the constraint of designing organizations that can be represented in the conventional tree. A "circular" organization can be both hierarchical and democratic. This type of organization is described in Chapter 9.

SUMMARY

In this chapter we considered how the range of variables said to be controllable in a problem situation can be increased. Creative solutions to problems often involve the selection of a course of action that was not initially among those thought to be available, but was subsequently revealed by the ways of thinking discussed in this chapter.

First, we observed that most of us come to a problem with a concept of relevancy that dictates what variables we consider. This concept derives from our education or, more particularly, from our discipline or profession. Each such conceptual "set" excludes the consideration of relevant controllable variables that are not excluded by some other "set." Therefore, I suggest the use of interdisciplinary and interprofessional teams in problem formulation.

Next, we observed that in many problems that arise out of a perceived deficiency, we look for a simple unitary cause, something to blame and try to supress, remove, or contain in some way. I suggest the consideration of the possibility of converting the "culprit" into a constructive force by adding something to the environment rather than subtracting something from it.

Many problems are the consequences of implicit or explicit manmade incentives that produce unintended and undesirable behavior by others. These incentives should be uncovered and examined. They can frequently be corrected in such a way as to dissolve the problem.

Problems that resist solution can often have their backs broken by enlarging the system we consider changing. *System* and *environment* are relative concepts; they are not "given" to us but are imposed *by* us on the field of our perception. Therefore, we can enlarge or contract either one. Our tendency is to contract them to cut problems down to manageable size. This may often preclude any solution, let alone a good one.

When a problem that arises out of a failure is one of a set of similar failure-based problems, a search for a common property of these failures can often reveal something subtle that can be controlled and that, if controlled, precludes future failures of the same type. The property common to the failures must, of course, not be present in any of the successes.

Problems that arise because of changing conditions and can be expected to continue because of continuing change can often be treated by the use of *reference projections*. Such projections are extrapolations from current trends assuming no intervention that will change them. Such projections are used to predict what *cannot*, rather than what *will*, happen. What will happen depends on what we do or fail to do between now and "then."

Many of the constraints that limit what we believe we can do in a problem situation are unconsciously self-imposed. By raising them to consciousness and questioning their validity, we can often find ways of removing or relaxing them. This can sometimes be done by finding new ways of using available technology, by developing new technology, or by using an indigenous technology that is overlooked because it is in a place we consider unlikely, for example, among the uneducated.

Finally, we tend to look for solutions where we find the problem. They may, however, lie in other places. Symptoms do not necessarily appear where their cause is located. We often think in geometrical terms, particularly about organizations, and our searches for solutions tend to be restricted by the dimensionality of our mental pictures. Such dimensionality is not inherent in the system and is therefore subject to our control. Increasing the number of dimensions in which we think about problems can often reveal new and more effective solutions.

In general, we try to simplify our problems by reducing the number of alternative solutions we consider. Simplifying problems can preclude solutions better than those we consider. The consequences of every simplifying assumption should therefore be seriously evaluated. *Simplification is often simple minded.*

CHAPTER FOUR

Uncontrolled Variables

Recall that the environment of a problem consists of the uncontrolled variables that affect the outcome of the course of action taken. These variables create the conditions and some of the constraints under which the problem must be solved. Recall also that variables uncontrolled by one person may be controlled by another. Furthermore, as I try to show, variables that a decision maker considers to be out of his control may actually be within it. Self-imposed constraints may convert a controllable variable into one that appears to be uncontrollable.

Determining the values of uncontrolled variables is an important part of problem formulation. In fact, the very existence of a problem, let alone its properties, depends on these values. For example, if my house were on fire, I would have a problem; if not, I would not. If my house were on fire, the location of the fire, its size and rate of growth, what was burning, what was near it, and so on would constitute what are called the *facts of the case*.

Among such facts are usually some we take to be self-evident. One should be wary of such facts. *Self-evident,* according to Ambrose Bierce (1911), the American wit, means: "Evident to one's self and to nobody else" (p. 318). Unfortunately, this is not true; others often take for granted what we take to be self-evident. *Self-evidence,* in practice, is what is usually accepted *without* evidence.

The reason for being wary of what appears to us or others as self-evident or *obvious* is revealed in the story of a mathematician who, when going through a proof of a theorem of geometry in class, said of one of his steps: "The reason for this, of course, is obvious." He went on to the next step, but stopped half-way through it, reexamined the previous step, scratched his head, and looked puzzled. Then he turned to the class and said, "Excuse me. I'll be right back." He left the classroom for his office and was gone for some time. Eventually he returned with a self-satisfied grin on his face and said, "I was right: that step is obvious."

This story is mirrored in another told about Norbert Wiener, the famous mathematician who fathered cybernetics. He was once required to teach an introductory course in the calculus. After a few sessions of the class, he told the students he could not stand teaching such elementary material. He announced that from then on he would present some of his recent work on harmonic analysis and Brownian motion. He also told the students to study the text, do the exercises at the end of each chapter, turn them in, and he would have them graded and returned.

Wiener then took off into the mathematical stratosphere and lost contact with the students who remained behind on the ground. Although they could hardly understand a word he said, they had a great time. It was like watching a good foreign film without subtitles. They liked the acting even if they could not follow the plot.

Unfortunately, about half-way through the course, the students learned that the final examination, on which their grades would depend completely, was departmentally prepared and administered. Their concern led them to plot Wiener's return to Earth. The brightest student in the class was selected to carry out the plan that was prepared collectively.

At the beginning of the next session of the class, before Wiener could get started, the class spokesman raised and waved his hand, breaking through Wiener's detachment from his environment. Wiener asked him what he wanted. He said that several of the students had had difficulty with one of the problems in the last set of exercises they had done. Would the professor be kind enough to go over it for them? Wiener grunted acquiescence and grabbed a copy of the text from the hand of a student sitting in the first row. He asked for the page and problem numbers, got them, turned to the problem, looked at it for a moment, went to the blackboard, and wrote "$x = y + z$." Then he said, "There's the answer," and tossed the book back to the student from whom he had taken it.

This, of course, was not exactly what the students wanted, but the bright young spokesman was very resourceful. He jumped to his feet and said, "Thank you, Professor Wiener. We appreciate your help. But, sir, I wonder if there is another way of doing that problem."

Wiener was visibly annoyed by this further invasion of his privacy but, reluctantly acknowledging his obligation to the class, went back to the student in the first row and took the book from him again. Once more he asked for the page and problem numbers, got them, turned to the problem, looked at it for a moment, went to the blackboard, and wrote "$x = y + z$." Then he said, "Yes, there is, and you can see they check."

More often than not *self-evident* and *obvious* signify facts whose truthfulness we are not willing to question, not facts whose truthfulness is unquestionable. It is important, therefore, to question the facts of the case whose truthfulness is accepted without evidence. The more self-evident or obvious such facts are, the more intensively they should be questioned. They often turn out to be false, and the discovery that they are false frequently reveals possible courses of action that were previously hidden. One of these courses of action may well be superior to any previously considered. Here are some cases in point.

Fable 4.1.   THE STEWARDESS TURNOVER PROBLEM.

Back in the 1950s a team of researchers of which Aesop was a part was trying to determine for a major domestic airline how often it should hire girls, conduct classes to train them to be stewardesses, and how large these classes should be. The attrition rate among stewardesses was high. Most of them left the airline within two years, usually for marriage. At that time stewardesses were not allowed to be married.

Those familiar with production-management problems will recognize this school-scheduling problem as a bizarre instance of the economic-lot-size (or production-run-size) problem. Stewardesses can be thought of as the output of a production process, the training sessions. Thus the problem could be stated as: How many stewardesses should be made how often?

A solution was found by Aesop and his colleagues that promised significant but not dramatic savings to the airline. In the process of finding the solution, however, Aesop and his associates learned that the average number of hours the stewardesses were in the air per month was considerably less than the maximum allowed under the relevant union contract. By questioning others they found out why few could fly the maximum allowable number of hours.

First, suppose all flights were eight hours long and that the maximum allowable flying time was one hundred hours. Then a stewardess could only be assigned to twelve flights which, if they took no more time than scheduled, would take (twelve × eight) ninety-six hours. Four hours would necessarily be lost; they would be "unavoidable scrap."

Second, suppose all flights were ten hours long and that ten of these were assigned to a stewardess. If any one of her first nine flights was delayed by more than a specified amount of time, a common occurrence, she would not be permitted to take her last scheduled flight. A reserve stewardess would have to be used. Therefore, some allowance (buffer) for the uncertainty of flight times was required.

Aesop and his colleagues then asked what was the maximum average flying time that could be obtained from stewardesses under these conditions. This was a very difficult question, but they were able to determine that about a fifty percent increase was theoretically possible. This encouraged them to try to find a way of combining flights into monthly stewardess assignments that, in practice, would realize most of the theoretically possible improvement. They found such a way, and it promised dramatic savings to the airline.

With considerable self-satisfaction Aesop presented these results at a meeting of the airline's department heads. All but one was enthusiastic about Aesop's unsolicited effort. The holdout was the director of personnel, who said that the procedure presented could not be used because it would make the stewardesses leave their jobs earlier than they would normally, and this would increase recruiting and training costs by more than Aesop's assignment procedure would save. He said that most stewardesses would refuse to fly as many hours as the proposed procedure would require of them.

Aesop was not prepared for this objection. The possibility of accelerated attrition had not occurred to him or his colleagues. Therefore, he felt obliged to save face by asking the director of personnel how he knew the stewardesses would react as he had said. The Director's reply was: "My God! Everybody knows this." Aesop pressed and asked him how *he* knew this. The director blurted out, "It's obvious to anyone who deals with stewardesses."

This was Aesop's call to arms. He asked for permission to investigate the truthfulness of this "fact," pointing out that it would take little time and effort. He was given permission to do so by all but the director of personnel, who said it would be a waste of time and money. The majority's permission prevailed, and Aesop went ahead.

At each of the airports that served as a stewardess base, an administrator used the next month's flight schedule to combine flights into stewardess assignments for the month. These "bids," as they were called, were typed on cards that were posted on a bulletin board. The most senior stewardess at the base had first choice. The next most senior stewardess had second choice, and so on. Thus it was possible to obtain records of the assignments and the choices made at each base. Using these data Aesop and his colleagues plotted the flying hours of the assignments selected against the seniority of the stewardess (see Figure 4.1).

If the director of personnel had been right, the plot would have followed a curve something like A, with the more senior girls selecting the assignments with the smallest number of flying hours. If he had been right I would not be telling this story. The data actually followed a curve like B. This was a surprise even to Aesop; he had expected to find no relationship. Therefore, he thought it desirable to find an explanation of what had been observed. An analysis of the differences between longer and shorter assignments revealed that the schedules with more flying hours provided greater regularity of days off and more off-duty time at the stewardess's home base. Aesop's team then revised their scheduling procedure to provide complete regularity of days off and to increase the amount of free time that could be spent in the base city. This was done with only a small reduction of the average flying hours obtained by the first assignment procedure. The results were much better than those yielded by the procedure then in use.

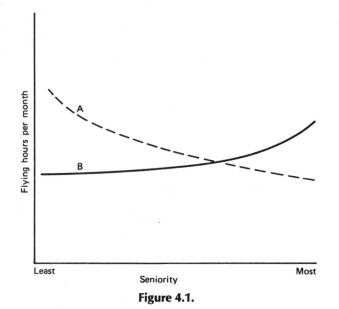

Figure 4.1.

Aesop presented the revised procedure and the results to both the stewardesses and the managers. Both enthusiastically accepted it, including the contrite director of personnel. The procedure was implemented successfully.

> **MORAL: There is nothing so deceptive as an apparent truth.**

A self-evident "fact" may not only prevent our seeeing an effective course of action that is available, but, as in this fable, it may preclude the consideration of a course of action that is known to be available. The more obvious a statement appears to be, the more thoroughly its truthfulness should be investigated. Unfortunately, the more obvious a "fact" appears to be, the more resistance there usually is to efforts to test it, as the next fable shows.

Fable 4.2.   THE BLACK PROBLEM IS WHITE.

A large public utility, most of whose operations are located in major cities, asked Aesop to work on the following problem. The proportion of its workers who were Black had recently passed forty percent and was increasing rapidly. The company expected that before the end of the 1970s a majority of its employees would be Black. On the other hand, less than one percent of its supervisory and managerial personnel were Black, and this percentage was not increasing. Therefore, some its managers saw the company becoming what they called a "corporate plantation."

The director of personnel wanted to increase the number of Blacks in supervision and management. To this end he asked Aesop to design an educational program for the company's Black employees that would increase their upward mobility.

Aesop began by asking for access to the personnel records of five hundred randomly selected Black employees and the same number of White employees drawn from those in the same types of job as the Blacks held. The personnel director explained that this would be very difficult because each employee's records were in three parts in three different locations; they would be very difficult to collect and collate. Aesop explained that he could not design an educational program for Black employees without knowing in detail their educational deficiencies, and he knew of no other feasible way of obtaining this information. The director of personnel told Aesop that he could safely assume

Fable 4.2. The black problem is white. Moral: Facts are easily colored by one's perspective.

the Blacks were deficient in every relevant way. This was an assumption Aesop was not willing to make, and, he explained, it had to be put into quantitative terms anyhow. Therefore, he pressed for access to the records. It was refused. Aesop then exercised his contractual right to discontinue the work.

Word of this dispute reached one of the parent company's executives, who was outraged. Because of pressure he brought to bear in the right places, Aesop was invited back and the records were made available to him. When he analyzed them, he found that Black female employees had an average of one and a half years more equivalent education than White female employees in the same types of job. Black males had an average of three-quarters of a year more equivalent education than White males in the same types of job.

On the basis of these findings, Aesop told the company that its problem was not one of educating Black employees for upward mobility, but of educating White supervisors and managers so they would permit Blacks to move up.

Aesop's suggestion was summarily rejected, and Aesop once again terminated his relationship with the company, this time permanently.

More than a year later a federal court found the company guilty of discriminatory practices against Black employees who had brought suit against the company.

> **MORAL: Facts are easily colored by one's perspective.**

Nothing is harder to topple than a "fact" that supports a deeply held prejudice denied by its holder.

It is not hard to understand why we take so many "facts" for granted and why we resist any effort to test them. These are usually "facts" we use to justify a course of action that we believe will produce a strongly desired outcome, one frequently defended on moral grounds. We then confuse the morality of our end with the validity of the facts on which our choice of means is based. Not every act performed with good intentions is a good act.

We tend to classify people into dichotomous categories: good and evil. We expect no good from the evil and no evil from the good. These expectations are seldom shaken by facts. For example, Americans find it difficult to find good in anything that the Russians do, and the Russians have the same difficulty with Americans. The use of stereotypes prevents our search for alternatives to the limited choice they permit. For example, a rural preacher in the deep South was urging members of his congregation to confess their sexual sins. He said, "I wants all you what's been he-in' and she-in' to rise and ask God's forgiveness." The majority of the congregation rose and did so. Then he said, "I wants all you what's been he-in' and he-in' or she-in' and she-in' to rise and ask God's forgiveness." All the rest rose except one young man seated conspicuously in the front row. When those who rose had finished asking for God's forgiveness, the preacher turned to the young man and asked, "What's the matter wif you? Ain't you been sinnin'?" The young man replied, "I has, but you ain't called on me yet. I been me-in' and me-in'."

An examination of one of our current environmental issues reveals how easily facts are manipulated to serve causes.

Many environmentalists who have focused on the solid waste and litter problems have tended to make nonreusable beverage containers their principal target. However, these containers make up only about three and a half percent of household-generated solid waste. The amount generated by households increases by about four percent per year. Therefore, even if all beverage containers were eliminated, it would not have a significant impact on the solid waste problem. On the other hand, beverage containers make up about twenty percent of litter, which is a more conspicuous, if less serious problem. Beverage containers are the most noted part of litter, and, unlike much of it, they do not decompose or blow away.

Legislation to ban, restrict, or penalize the use of nonreusable beverage containers has been proposed to hundreds of legislative bodies at every level of government. One of the principal arguments put forward in support of such proposals is that they would reduce solid waste. It seems obvious that if a container is reused it does not contribute to solid waste. This seems so obvious it requires no evidence to support it. Let's see.

The amount of solid waste is measured by its *weight,* not the number of items in it, and for good reason. The cost of its collection and disposal is much more closely related to its weight than to the number of items. For example, it costs no more to dispose of a shredded newspaper than one that is left intact. Therefore, the number of beverage containers in solid waste is not nearly as important as is the total weight.

Returnable bottles are about fifty percent heavier than one-way bottles and from five to fifteen times heavier than cans, depending on the material of which the cans are made. Returnable bottles are about four times as heavy as the weighted average of all one-way containers. Therefore, unless they are used four times or more, their exclusive use would increase the amount of solid waste.

Current data indicate that reusable containers are reused considerably more than four times. Therefore, the argument still appears to be sound. But let us go a bit further.

About eighty-five percent of the reusable beer containers are used at places that serve beer on their premises, for example, bars and restaurants. These have a high return rate. Those returnable containers used off the premises at which they are purchased average only about four trips. Therefore, the off-premise use of returnable beer containers currently generates as much solid waste per unit of beverage as do one-way containers. However, those who use returnable containers today do so *voluntarily;* they have a choice. If legislation banning the use of one-way containers were enacted, most of the users of these containers would be doing so *in*voluntarily. It is not unlikely that they would return containers less frequently than those who use them now by choice. Therefore, such legislation could result in an increase in solid waste.

To some people who have paid attention to the facts I have just reviewed, there is a simple and obvious response: increase the deposit of reusable containers until an adequate return rate is obtained. However, experiments on doing just this have failed to produce significant increases in return rates. Furthermore, if the deposit were greater than the cost of the container—for example, ten cents—this would stimulate the production of containers just for return, and doing so would be legal. This would, in turn, raise the cost of containers and the beverage, which would reduce consumption and government income from taxes on beer.

Let us return to the environmental objective: to find more efficient and effective ways of collecting and disposing of solid waste and of reclaiming and reusing as much of it as economically feasible. Most solid waste collection and disposal systems in the United States are "archaic" and operate below current standards set by the federal government, but few communities can afford to replace the old systems with new and better ones. The critical need, therefore, is to provide communities with funds they can use to improve their systems and finance development of even better systems than those currently available. In addition, there is a need for an incentive that will increase consciousness of solid waste among producers and consumers. These two considerations lead to the suggestion of a tax on *all* items that contribute to solid waste, a tax equal to their cost of collection and disposal. These costs would then be paid by users and not the public at large. Income generated by such a tax could be used to upgrade current solid waste systems and to finance the development of better ones. The tax would also increase solid waste consciousness and therefore is likely to lead to more rational behavior by both producers and consumers.

Research has shown that the tax rate required would be about one cent per pound. This converts to a tax of one-quarter cent per beverage container. A similar approach can and has been taken to the litter problem (see John R. Hall, et al., 1971).

There are no simple or obvious facts on which to base a simple and obvious solution to complex problems. The loftiness of our ends does not by itself endow the means we propose for pursuing these ends with either effectiveness or efficiency. Nor does it endow the facts on which our means are based with validity.

The conceptualization of a problematic situation is a synthesis of the relevant facts of the case. Such a conceptualization does not follow mechanically from these facts. Interpretation of the facts is always present, and interpretation is always subjective, reflecting one's assumptions and self-imposed constraints.

For example, a young man came into a psychiatrist's office and introduced himself. Before the psychiatrist could respond, the young man said, "I want to make it perfectly clear before we begin that I am here against my will. My family insisted on it."

"Why did they insist on it?" the psychiatrist asked.

"They think I'm peculiar because I insist I'm dead."

The psychiatrist hid his surprise and asked calmly, "Do you know anyone else who is dead?"

"No. I'm the only one I know who's dead."

The psychiatrist reflected for a moment and then asked the young man, "Dead people don't bleed, do they?"

The young man said, "No."

The psychiatrist told the young man to take off his jacket and roll up one of his shirt sleeves. The young man followed the instructions, but asked why he was so instructed.

Before an answer could be provided the psychiatrist had drawn an empty syringe from his desk, inserted it into the young man's arm, and pulled the plunger out, filling the chamber of the syringe with the young man's blood.

The young man watched this with amazement and then blurted out: "By God, dead people do bleed. Don't they?"

So much for facts of the case.

"The whole is greater than the sum of its parts" is a familiar adage. Unfortunately, we often ignore some of its implications. For example, a collection of courses of action each of which, when considered separately, is infeasible, may nevertheless be feasible as a whole. There is a surprising and useful consequence of this property of interdependent actions: the constraints imposed on us by one uncontrolled variable may be removed by making relevant a previously irrelevant uncontrolled variable. Thus some problems can be solved more easily and effectively by increasing the number of relevant uncontrolled variables.

This principle is commonly used in management decisions to "integrate vertically." For example, a company that uses agricultural products as its raw material and whose profits are out of control because of wide swings in the cost of these products, may go into farming, growing its own raw materials. By so doing it may reduce the fluctuations of its overall profits, since the two swings tend to cancel each other.

Although vertical integration is a common way of controlling one uncontrolled variable by the use of another, "horizontal integration"—*coordination*—is not, but it may yield equally effective results. Here is an example.

Fable 4.3.   ONE FOR THE ROAD.

A company that manufactured machine tools was periodically plagued by large shifts in demand for its products. When the economy was on the way up, sales of its products increased more rapidly than the economy; when the economy slumped, its sales dropped even faster. These swings made it difficult to operate the company's plant efficiently. Therefore, a better and longer-range forecast of sales seemed essential for smoothing production and reducing its cost. The chief executive of the company asked Aesop to develop such a forecast.

Aesop worked long and hard to develop a suitable forecasting procedure, but to no avail. Only after he felt he had hit a blank wall did he sit back and rethink the nature of the problem. The objective was to smooth demand for products; improved forecasting was a means for living with irregular demand. This suggested an alternative approach: how could the company's product line be modified to dissolve the problem? This could be done by adding a line of products that had a demand cycle that ran counter to that of machine tools and used the same technology of production.

Once the problem was defined in this way, Aesop's search for a suitable product was relatively easy. A type of road-building equipment was found that fitted the bill. The company followed Aesop's suggestion through an acquisition. Although each product line's demand fluctuated in an unpredictable way, together they provided a considerably smoothed demand that made it possible to produce both types of product more economically than either could be produced alone.

MORAL: In some cases $1 + 1 = 0$.

Stories of this type are common in business circles. I can remember hearing years ago about a company that made rubber contraceptives and nipples for baby bottles. It did not care which way things went. The familiar term for such a strategy is *hedging*.

Another simple example of combining several "bad" things to get one good one arose in the dairy business.

Fable 4.4.   THE SOUR MILKMAN.

The chief executive of a company that produced dairy products and delivered them to the home by the familiar but vanishing milkman found the company's costs of delivery rising rapidly. As he increased prices to cover these costs, the company became less competitive with retail stores, particularly supermarkets. Fewer and fewer households were willing to pay as much as was required for the convenience of home delivery. Sales decreased, and delivery costs escalated further.

It was no secret that most businesses that depended on regular home delivery were in similar straits. This suggested two possible solutions to the problem. One involved the cooperation of competing companies in forming a kind of "United Home Delivery Service" so that one milkman could deliver many brands, but to customers close to each other. This would decrease delivery costs considerably, but the company rejected this suggestion because it considered its drivers to be salesmen whom it wanted to control.

The second alternative was accepted. It involved extending the product line to include fruit drinks, baked goods, and a selection of staple foods so that the average size of a delivery could be increased. Each of these products taken separately could not make it with home delivery, but collectively they could and did.

> **MORAL: Even a milk pitcher needs a good delivery
> to home plates.**

Combining deficiencies may also solve problems of physical design. Here is an example.

Fable 4.5.   THE UPSIDE-DOWN STORY.

A manufacturer of refrigerators had a persistent problem arising from the fact that each model had to be produced in two versions, one with right-hand doors and the other with left-hand doors. The numbers of each version of a model that were bought in different markets varied considerably and significantly from year to year. Thus sales by door type could not be predicted accurately. As a result, stocks were out of balance in many markets, some with too many right-hand doors, and

Fable 4.5. The upside-down story. Moral: It's a good idea to know which side one's door is butted on.

others with too many left-hand doors. This led to both lost sales and excessive inventories.

Aesop was called in to develop better forecasting of the sales of the two versions. It immediately occurred to him that if a refrigerator could be opened from either side, the problem would disappear. He was quickly informed that another manufacturer had built such a door, hinged in the center of its top and bottom, and it had flopped. It was expensive, and ambidexterity had little or no value to the customer.

Nevertheless, Aesop felt the idea was worth pursuing. One day he noted that if the door of the refrigerator made by the company was turned upside down, its outer side looked exactly the same except that the handle was on the other side. He learned that this was deliberate; right- and left-hand doors were the same except for their hinging. Furthermore, the door and the shelves mounted into the back of the door were so designed that the shelves could also be inserted upside down. This led Aesop to design a refrigerator door frame that had hinge receptacles on both sides. Those on the side not in use could be covered with a snap-on plate. The hinges themselves were designed to snap into the receptacles. This meant that the same door could be mounted on either side; furthermore, it could be changed at any time before or after purchase. The additional cost of production was very small compared to the cost of additional inventory and lost sales resulting from the traditional design. Aesop's design also offered the customer convertibility, should it be required by a move or remodelling.

> **MORAL:** **It's a good idea to know which side one's door is butted on.**

In combining uncontrolled variables to gain control over a situation, we enlarge the system under consideration. As noted previously, it is more common to reduce the situation under consideration—"cut it down to size"—than to enlarge it. Enlargement can often open up new possibilities for solution. Here is a case in point.

Fable 4.6.   THE DOUBLE-DECKED BUSSING PROBLEM.

There is a research institute in Europe with which Aesop had collaborated over many years. On one of his visits to this institute to discuss a project on which they were working together, he stopped in to see one of his old friends. During their exchange of greetings it was apparent to Aesop that his friend was preoccupied; Aesop asked him what was bothering him. He told Aesop he was stuck on a problem. Aesop suggested he describe the problem and the difficulty because doing so might help him reorganize his thinking about it. His friend agreed. This is the story he told.

A large European city uses double-decker busses as its principal means of public transportation. Each bus has a crew of two: a driver who occupies a cab separated from the rest of the bus, and a conductor who has three functions. He signals the driver when there are passengers who want to get off at the next stop, he signals him again when he is free to start, and he collects fares from those who have boarded. Fares are normally collected when the bus is in motion to make the stops as short as possible. During peak hours this often requires the conductor to force his way through the crowd on both levels and the stairs so he can collect fares. He frequently fails to return to the entrance in time to signal the driver to stop or not. The driver then has to stop, often when there are no passengers to be discharged. Such unnecessary stops bred hostility between driver and conductor, a hostility that was augmented by the incentive system under which they operated.

To encourage the busses to run on time, an incentive system had been developed that paid drivers a bonus for being on time. There was also an incentive system for conductors to ensure their collecting fares from everyone. Plain-clothes inspectors frequently rode the busses and checked to see if the conductor got all the fares. If not, he was penalized.

No wonder that in several cases a driver became so angry at his conductor that he stopped the bus between stops, got out of his cab, went to the rear, pulled the conductor off the bus, and beat him up. After several such incidents their separate unions became involved and declared war on each other. Violence prevailed.

It was at this point that Aesop's friend had been called in. He was committed to the principle of participative problem solving and had arranged a set of meetings of small groups of drivers and conductors in which they were supposed to discuss ways of resolving their differences, including changes in the incentive system. Almost all these sessions ended in violence. None yielded constructive results.

Having completed his description of the situation, Aesop's friend asked him if he had any ideas. Aesop said he did not, but that he had a few questions. Aesop asked how many busses were in operation at peak hours and how many stops there were in the system. Aesop's friend told him it would take some time to get the answers, and he could not see what good they would do once obtained. Aesop said the answers would enable him to get a sense of the size of the system involved. His friend said the size of the system was irrelevant because the problem arose *within* the bus. Aesop agreed but pointed out that the solution might lie outside it. Although not convinced, his friend agreed to go ahead.

The data showed that there were more busses in operation at peak hours than there were stops. (Those who have been on Fifth Avenue in New York City at peak hours have seen such a state.)

This information immediately suggested a solution to Aesop: during peak hours the conductors be located at the stops, not on the busses. Then they could collect fares from passengers while they were waiting for a bus. Conductors could signal drivers when to start by using a button located at the rear entrance to the bus, and passengers could signal the driver when they wanted to get off by pulling a cord around the sides of the bus. Not only would this reduce delays, it would also make fare collection easier. When the number of busses in operation was less than the number of stops, at off hours, the conductor could return to the bus.

MORAL: Striking a conductor is not fare play.

This solution was developed and eventually implemented in several cities. On reflection it becomes apparent that this type of solution is already in use in subway systems.

A symptom may appear in any part of a system even though its source may be in any other part or in their interactions. We do not treat headaches by performing brain surgery.

We may fail to solve a problem not only because we take as irrelevant or uncontrollable a variable that we can actually control, but also because we assume *others* cannot control one or more variables that they actually can. Here is an example.

**Fable 4.7.   WHEN YOU CAN'T GO FORWARD,
            BACK UP.**

In the 1950s one urban university, like many others, had a serious parking problem on its campus. There was not enough space on its parking lots to accommodate all the cars driven to the campus by faculty, students, and service personnel. The university was firmly committed to providing free parking because of the lack of adequate public transportation.

Many latecomers parked "illegally" in the aisles of the parking lots rather than park off campus and walk a considerable distance. This prevented others from leaving the campus when they wanted to. Complaints mounted in number and intensity, forcing a response from the university's administrators. After considering several alternative systems, they selected one and had it installed. It required the registration of cars with on-campus parking rights. Since there was not enough space for all, a priority system was used.

Fable 4.7. When you can't go forward, back up. Moral: It is often harder to solve a problem created by others than it is for them to solve the problem created by the solution.

Those who were registered were given a plastic card which, when inserted in a receptacle at the entrance to assigned lots, opened the arm that blocked the entrance. After entering, the car crossed a treadle in the road which lowered the arm behind it. A similar arm blocked the exit except that it was activated by passing over a treadle before the gate. It was closed by a treadle outside the gate.

Those students who were deprived of on-campus parking by this system easily found a way to beat it. Within a few days several of them were producing and selling counterfeit cards. As a result, within a short time the lots were just as abused as they had been before the installation of the new system. Complaints arose with renewed vigor.

The responsible authorities went to work again, this time to make the system fool (sic!) proof. They made three costly changes in the system. First, a counter was connected to the arm-closing treadle at the entrance. It counted the number of cars that entered. Second, a similar counter was installed at the exit, connected to the arm-closing treadle there. It counted the number of cars that left. Third, a small computer calculated the number of cars on the lot by taking the difference between those entered and those left, and locked the entrance when capacity was reached.

All this was intended to prevent anyone from entering a lot that was full. However, the students discovered very quickly that if they backed up over the treadle that closed the exit gate, a car was counted out of the lot. Then they would be admitted at the entrance. The lots were once again saturated.

The administrators, now more dedicated to their task than ever, responded by connecting the exit counter to the arm-opening treadle inside the lot. The students found that by jumping on this treadle a car would be counted out.

At this point the administration gave up and placed a guard at the entrance of each lot.

> **MORAL:** **It is often harder to solve a problem cre-
> ated by others than it is for them to solve
> the problem created by the solution.**

The way a person who has a problem thinks about it is usually quite different from the way that those who cause the problem think about it. For this reason military systems designers have long used what are called "countermeasure groups." These are teams of highly competent researchers who are asked to play the "enemy," but, unlike the enemy, they are given all the information they want. Their objective is to find out how to beat the system. When they find a way to do so, they reveal it to the system designers, who then alter their design to counter the countermeasure. Then the countermeasure group goes at it again. This process is continued until a design is produced that will accomplish its mission despite the efforts of the countermeasure group. Although this procedure does not guarantee success with a "real enemy," it greatly increases chances for it.

If the parking lot problem described in the last fable had been given to a student countermeasure group, it would have revealed how the system could be beaten before its installation rather than afterwards.

The behavior of others is often the least yielding type of uncontrolled variable, but this is so because we usually do not provide them with proper incentives. We already considered (in Chapter 3) how incentives can and should be brought under control. They are a potentially powerful means of bringing the uncontrolled behavior of others under control, even when the others are autonomous. The next fable illustrates this point.

Fable 4.8.   THE COMPANY THAT BOUGHT BIDED TIME.

A company that produced a line of products widely used in a variety of manufacturing processes had enjoyed a rapid growth in sales volume over a relatively short period of time. Its profits, however, had increased very slowly. The principal reason for this was found to be very large increase in its finished-goods inventory held in about one hundred and fifty company-operated warehouses. Purchasers either came to these warehouses to pick up what they needed or deliveries were made to them.

An internal research team was given the problem of reducing these inventories. Some well-known mathematical procedures were applied, and some improvement was obtained, but considerably less than was hoped for.

The responsible manager believed the research team must have made a mistake or used less than the best analytical procedure. Therefore, he called on Aesop to review what his team had done.

Aesop conducted the review, but found nothing wrong in what the team had done. However, he did observe that the typical size of an order for the company's products was very small, usually only enough to meet a few days' requirement of a customer. Because it is a well-known characteristic of inventory that it tends to decrease as orders either increase in size or decrease in frequency, Aesop asked why the company did not offer a quantity discount to encourage larger and less frequent purchases by its customers. He was told that it had offered such a discount but that it had not worked, for good reason. The material produced by the company deteriorated when stored under normal atmospheric conditions. It required humidity-controlled storage to prevent deterioration. The company's warehouses were so controlled, but this was not true of the storage areas in its customers' plants. Therefore, they would lose much of what they bought if they had to store it for more than a few days.

Aesop could see no easy way out of this difficulty. He then used a trick he had often found useful in such difficult problem situations: he modified the problem to make it as difficult as he could. Making the problem even harder to solve often reveals a course of action previously overlooked.

The worst form of the problem Aesop could imagine would occur if each customer picked up or had delivered only one item at a time. Then the warehouses would have to operate much as retail stores. Once the problem was formulated this way, Aesop was able to see a possibility he had previously overlooked. If what each customer would want was known long enough ahead of time, the warehouses could be stocked to known demand. Then, however small the orders, inventories could be considerably reduced. Therefore, he turned his attention to how he could induce customers to place their orders as far in advance of their need as possible.

Aesop found that most customers' purchasing agents knew what their requirements would be well ahead of time, but there was no reason for them to share this information with the supplier. Aesop sought to give them one.

He determined how much the company would save if various percentages of its customers could be induced to place their orders various amounts of time before delivery or pickup was required. The potential savings were very large. Therefore, Aesop proposed that half the savings be passed on to the customer in the form of an "advance-notice" discount: the more time between placing an order and its delivery or pickup, the lower its price would be.

This incentive scheme was implemented with considerable success.

> **MORAL:** **Splitting a difference can bring things to-gether.**

This fable has a number of points, but the one of central interest here is that it involves bringing an uncontrolled "external" variable—customer purchasing behavior—under partial control by the use of an internally generated incentive for customers.

The ability to use incentives to modify the behavior of others depends critically on how well their behavior is understood. In general, we do not understand their behavior as well as we think we do. This often precludes creative problem solving. A case in point is developed in Chapter 11. It is rather complex, but it illustrates well both the difficulty of gaining understanding of human behavior and its value once obtained.

CONCLUSION

The various morals and points made in this chapter can be summarized in three general observations.

First, in every problematic situation there is a set of relevant facts of the case. Some of these usually appear to be obvious. The more obvious such a fact appears to be, the more intensely its truth should be investigated. We are more likely to be wrong in what we accept without evidence, no matter how obvious it may be, than in what we accept with evidence, no matter how doubtful it may be. When an obvious fact of the case is toppled, it almost invariably opens opportunities for finding more creative and effective solutions to the problem in hand. It does so by converting what appeared to be an uncontrolled variable into one that is perceived to be controllable.

Second, uncontrolled variables often both create the problem confronted and constrain the actions that the decision maker can take to solve it. It is often possible to remove the problem or the constraints by enlarging the system taken to be relevant. This can convert uncontrolled into controlled variables. One uncontrolled variable can often be used to cancel the harmful effect of another. This is the principle behind the vertical and horizontal integration of organizations.

Third, many uncontrolled variables are not intrinsically uncontrollable. Lack of control over them does not lie in the nature of the variable but in our lack of knowledge and understanding of it. Therefore, research directed at producing relevant knowledge and understanding can often bring an uncontrolled variable under control. Part of the art of problem solving lies in knowing when and how to use such research.

CHAPTER FIVE

Relations

The way that a course of action affects the outcome of a problematic situation depends on how the relevant variables are interrelated and how they relate to the outcome. The belief that a variable is significantly related to the outcome of what we do is what makes us consider it relevant. Therefore, the selection of the variables that we attempt to manipulate and the way we attempt to manipulate them are determined by what we believe to be the nature of these relationships.

Causality is the most important type of relationship involved in problem solving. We seek to do things that will *bring about* a desired state. To "bring about" something is to cause it in either a strong sense—that is, to do something that completely *determines* the outcome—or a weak sense—to do something that may or may not affect or influence the outcome. A weak (probabilistic or nondeterministic) cause is sometimes referred to as a *producer* and its effect as a *product*. A producer (for example, an acorn) has some probability of producing its product (an oak) but is not certain to do so. In most "real" situations we deal with weak causal relationships. Strong causality usually requires laboratory or laboratory-like conditions.

Our ability to solve problems depends critically on how well we conceptualize the causal connections between what we do and what we want. Many of our problem-solving failures derive from assuming a causal connection where it does not exist or incorrectly characterizing a causal connection where it does exist. Perhaps the most common single cause of failure in problem solving derives from incorrectly assuming a causal relationship between variables that have only been demonstrated to be *associated*. Variables that tend to change together, in the same or opposite directions, are associated.

For example, the weight and height of persons are clearly associated. This means that if we obtain the weight and height of each of a sample of people and plot them on a graph, the points tend to increase together. Such an association is said to be positive. If an increase in one variable is associated with a decrease in the other—for example, income and illness—the association is said to be negative.

When two variables are associated, either can be used to predict the value of the other. For example, we can use the association of weight and height to predict one if we know the other. However, we *cannot* infer from their association that a change in weight will produce a change in height.

I have used weight and height because the error of causal inference is so apparent. This type of error is not always so apparent, and is therefore made over and over again. For example, suppose we plot a company's annual sales for a number of years against its annual advertising expenditures over the same years. Such plots often show a positive association between these two variables: sales and advertising expenditures tend to increase together. It does *not* follow, however, that an increase in advertising will produce an increase in sales. Advertising may have an effect on sales, as shown in Chapter 10, but even if it does, a positive association between sales and advertising does not prove it. Payroll and sales are usually positively associated; nevertheless it would be incorrect to infer that an increase in payroll will produce an increase in sales.

If there is no association between two variables, we can justifiably infer that they are *not* causally related *under the conditions in which the observations are made,* but not under other conditions. However, if there is an association, we should not infer that they are causally connected, that either is the cause of the other. The most we can infer is that they *may* be so related. Therefore, we can use association to filter a large number of variables to determine which should be studied further for causal relations.

The most commonly used measures of association are *correlation* and *regression* coefficients. The nature of these measures is not important here, but the cautious problem solver will remember that they are measures of association and therefore cannot legitimately be used for inferring causality. Caution is required because there are a number of widely used sophisticated statistical techniques such as factor and cluster analysis in which the fact that they are based on correlation or regression is very well concealed, often even from those who use them.

We can see the danger of inferring causality from association by returning to the advertising example. Suppose we plotted annual sales against advertising expenditures in the *following* year. In most cases in which I have done just this, I obtained a stronger positive association than that obtained when the same year was used. Clearly, we cannot infer that an increase in next year's advertising will increase this year's sales. In fact, if there is a causal connection between these variables it may well run in the opposite direction.

Many companies set their advertising budgets as a relatively fixed percentage of forecasted sales. Most sales-forecasting procedures are such that if there is an increase in sales one year, a further increase is likely to be forecast for the following year. Now we can see the causal sequence: if sales went up last year the company probably forecast an increase in sales this year. If it forecast such an increase, it probably increased advertising expenditures. Therefore, what this shows is that an increase in sales one year tends to produce an increase in advertising in the following year.

One cannot overestimate the frequency with which the erroneous inference of causality from association is made. Here are two examples of such errors made in problem areas that are currently considered to be very critical.

Fable 5.1. SMOKING PREVENTS CHOLERA.

Early in the war against cancer the medical profession's battle against smoking began. Numerous studies were published showing that smoking and lung cancer were positively associated. This could not be contradicted, but the inference drawn from such studies—that smoking causes cancer—could be. Again, smoking *may* be a cause of lung cancer, but their correlation is not an adequate basis for asserting that it is.

One study published in a prominent medical journal showed a strong positive correlation between per capita consumption of tobacco and the incidence of lung cancer over a number of countries. A causal connection was incorrectly inferred. To show that this was the case, Aesop used the same data on per capita consumption of tobacco for the same countries but substituted the incidence rate of cholera. He obtained a negative correlation that was stronger than the positive correlation revealed in the article. Using the same logic as that which appeared in the original article, Aesop prepared another article almost identical to the original except for the conclusion; he concluded that smoking prevents cholera. He submitted this article to the same medical journal in which the original article had appeared. It was rejected because, according to the referees, it was *facetious*. Aesop wrote to the editor admitting that he had been facetious, but then, was this not true of the original article? Why, he asked, had it been published? He received no reply.

> **MORAL: Where there's smoking, emotions are likely to be on fire.**

The commitment of medical researchers to reduce smoking blinds them not only to errors in inferential logic but also to other associations between variables that weaken their case. For example, a study conducted in England showed a strong positive association between the discontinuation of smoking and the incidence of mental illness. If we used the same erroneous logic as is used in so much medical research, we would infer that smoking prevents mental illness. Perhaps it does, but such an association as has been revealed does not establish the fact.

It is possible, of course, to get rid of a bad thing for the wrong reasons. This, however, does not validate the reasoning. Here is an example.

Fable 5.2.   BREATHING CAUSES TUBERCULOSIS.

A number of years ago researchers in the public health department of a major American city carried out the following study. They divided their city into sections of equal areas and then determined the annual amount of soot fall and per capita incidence of tuberculosis in each area. They found a strong positive correlation and concluded that soot fall caused tuberculosis. On the "strength" of their data they prepared and promoted a smoke-abatement ordinance that was eventually put into effect. After considerable public and private expenditure, the air was cleaned, but there was no reduction of tuberculosis.

A group of medical researchers in another city heard of this effort and decided to look into it. They knew of no medical connection between soot fall and tuberculosis, but they knew of evidence linking tuberculosis to dietary deficiencies.

Their research uncovered the following causal chain. People with low incomes live in low-rent districts. The more soot that falls in a district, the less desirable it is, hence the lower is the rent within it. Therefore, a higher percentage of low-income people live in high soot fall areas than middle- or upper-income people. Low-income families suffer from dietary deficiencies more than high-income families. Some

Fable 5.2. Breathing causes tuberculosis. Moral: Variables, like people, are often illegitimately charged with guilt by association.

types of dietary deficiency induce tuberculosis. Therefore, those who live in high soot fall areas are more likely to get tuberculosis than others, but soot fall is *not* the cause.

> **MORAL:** Variables, like people, are often illegiti-
> mately charged with guilt by association.

Few people, if any, are immune to inferring guilt by association. In the fable that follows my own lack of immunity is apparent.

Fable 5.3.   SUGAR IS SWEETER BUT PROTEIN IS NEATER.

A group of us at the university were doing research for a multinational firm one of whose principal product lines consisted of candies. In the early stages of this work we learned that per capita consumption of candy and its rate of change varied greatly from country to country. As might have been expected, we also found that these levels and rates of change were very similar to those for sugar in the same countries. This led us to believe that we would better understand candy consumption if we better understood sugar consumption. Therefore, we embarked on a search for such understanding.

We focused on the fact that per capita sugar consumption in England was higher than that in the United States. This was consistent with my observations made while living in England in the early 1960s. The British preoccupation with "sweets" is conspicuous even to a casual observer. For example, television commercials for candy are often addressed to adults and are intended to give the impression that candy is a substitute for sex.

My only complaint about England was the lack of heat in buildings (a deficiency that has since been largely removed). On waking in the morning my family and I would rush outdoors to warm up. For much of the year we were always cold. Consequently, it seemed to me that England's consumption of sugar and low interior temperatures could be connected. I hypothesized that sugar provided the fuel used by the body to maintain its temperature.

An examination of sugar consumption data for a number of nations revealed a negative association between sugar consumption and average temperature: the colder the climate the more sugar was consumed—for the countries for which we had data.

I was excited by this discovery and could hardly wait to reveal it publicly. The first opportunity I had to do so was in a talk I had been invited to give to a group of corporate executives at Columbia University. In the discussion that followed the revelation of my discovery, a member of the audience, the director of research for a large pharmaceutical company, made two observations. First, he said that sugar is known *not* to serve as a source of body heat, and, second, that Eskimos had a very low sugar consumption rate for obvious reasons, and some populations in the tropics had a high consumption rate. I felt like a fool.

Afterwards I met and spoke with my critic and found that, although he knew my explanation was wrong, he had no alternative to offer, but he offered to help in my search for one.

With his help, my colleagues and I began to look about for explanatory clues. The first one we ran across was contained in some research done at the Tavistock Institute of Human Relations in London. A study had been conducted there to determine the effects of the traditional tea break on industrial workers. This research had been carried out in response to a dispute between English industrial management and labor over the continuation of the tea break. Management wanted to eliminate it, and the workers did not.

A Tavistock team had taken readings of blood sugar levels of workers at regular intervals over the work day. Blood sugar is known to be a source of energy. The team found that the average English worker's blood sugar reached a peak shortly after a meal and then declined rapidly with work until after the next intake of food or beverage. At just about tea time, the workers' blood sugar was at a very low level and needed replenishment if they were to work at an acceptable pace. The sugar taken in their tea break beverages and in the accompanying sweets was quickly converted into blood sugar.

Because blood sugar levels varied among workers, the Tavistock researchers suspected that their diet was relevant. They found that blood sugar decreased most rapidly among workers on a high carbohydrate diet. It was this finding that directed our search for an explanation of sugar consumption. We found a study of the relationship between blood sugar and the amount of carbohydrate or protein consumed at breakfast by Americans. It showed that with a high carbohydrate breakfast, blood sugar reached a peak quickly but declined rapidly thereafter. With a high protein breakfast, blood sugar rose more slowly to a lower peak, but it declined more slowly and never got as low, before the next meal, as it did with a high carbohydrate breakfast.

This suggested that a high protein diet reduced the need for the replenishment of blood sugar between meals and therefore the need and desire for sugar which converts rapidly to blood sugar. The research that followed gave support to this hyothesis. Not only did the nature of national diets partially explain sugar consumption, but it also explained why children, who generally have a higher carbohydrate to protein ratio in their diets than adults and use more energy than adults, consume more sugar and sweets than adults.

MORAL: Sugar is sweet but not a source of heat.

The tendency to draw causal inferences from associations of variables is hard to resist, but such resistance is worth the effort. This does not mean that association should not be sought or used; they should be, but as *clues* with which to begin, not to conclude, searches for causes. The next fable illustrates this point.

Fable 5.4.   THE FILL-UP STATIONS THAT WERE NOT FULL UP.

A major national oil company opened several hundred new service stations each year. The number of these stations that turned out to be unprofitable or less than acceptably profitable was increasing. The company called on its marketing research unit to find out how to stem this tide.

The research team's members interviewed a large number of people in the company who supposedly knew something about service station performance. They were asked to identify those characteristics of service stations which they believed had a significant effect on performance. Considerably more than one hundred variables were thus identified, including such things as the size of the station, the number of attendants and pumps, the proximity of competition, price, the number of cars passing the station, and so on.

The research team then systematically determined which of these variables were correlated with service station performance by collecting and analyzing data from several hundred stations. Thirty-five variables were found to be significantly associated with station performance. These variables were used in an equation that was constructed to predict the sales of a service station once its site had been selected and its design completed. The use of this equation enabled the company to reduce the number of unsuccessful service stations it built, but the reduction obtained fell far short of what the company had hoped for.

Aesop was called in for help. He was exposed to a detailed description of the previous work. He reacted by pointing out that an equation based on associations between variables rather than causal relations could not *explain*, however well it predicted. He argued that to increase the company's effectiveness in selecting sites and designing stations, he would have to determine *why* people selected the service stations they did; that is, he would have to explain customers' behavior.

Aesop decided to focus his attention initially on the relationship between traffic and service station sales, because, he said, the only thing he was sure of was that if there were no cars going by a station it would have no sales. He also decided that, because most of the company's stations were located on corners formed by two intersecting city streets, he would concentrate on these.

Fable 5.4. The fill-up stations that were not full up. Moral: The less we understand something, the more variables we require to explain it.

Since there are four ways to enter and four ways to leave an unrestricted intersection, there are sixteen routes through it, including going back in the direction one came from, for example, after getting gas. Aesop selected a sample of 200 stations and counted the number of cars passing each station in each of the sixteen routes and the number in each route that stopped for service. The data thus obtained revealed that four routes yielded most of the customers, for example, the route that involved a right-hand turn around the station and the one that was straight through with the station on the car side at the far corner of the intersection.

Using the information he had collected, Aesop was able to construct an equation for predicting service station performance using only the number of cars in the four important routes and the percentages of cars in each that stopped for service. The average error of the predictions yielded by this equation was only one-third as large as that of the predictions yielded by the equation constructed by the company's marketing research team. However, this was not the end of Aesop's work; it was only the beginning.

Next, he sought an explanation of the fact that four particular routes yielded most of the customers and an explanation of the percentages yielded by each. An examination of the routes suggested that they were the ones that involved least *lost time* in stopping for service.

Aesop set about testing this hypothesis by having cars that did and did not stop timed through the intersection. This enabled him to calculate the average time lost by cars stopping for service in each route. When he ordered the routes from the one with the least lost time to the one with the most, the order was exactly the same as that obtained by ordering the routes from the one with the largest percentage of cars stopping for service to the one with the smallest percentage. Now he felt he was on the track of an explanation of customer behavior, but he still did not have one.

A plot of the percentage of cars stopping in each route against the average time lost by stopping revealed that the percentage decreased proportionally to the square of the time; for example, only one-quarter as many cars stopped when lost time doubled. This suggested that "perceived lost time" was the critical causal variable, because psychological experiments have shown that perceived time—when it is not used to do something of interest—increases as the square of clock time.

Aesop then designed experiments to test his causal hypothesis. For example, he found that "waiting for an attendant" was a large component of lost time. Therefore, in a selected set of stations Aesop arranged for the attendants, when not otherwise occupied, to stand conspicuously in front of the pumps. Using his causal hypothesis, Aesop predicted the effect of this change on the percentage of cars stopping at these stations. These predictions turned out to be quite accurate.

By this and similar experiments Aesop confirmed his explanation of service station performance. This explanation, based on perceived lost time, not only yielded predictions that enabled the company to reduce the number of unsuccessful service stations to an acceptable level, but it also enabled the company to modify many of the stations that had been built earlier to improve their performances significantly.

MORAL: The less we understand something, the
more variables we require to explain it.

Causal inferences require the establishment of more than associations;
they require the demonstration that in some specified environment
either a change in the product cannot occur unless there is a preceding
or simultaneous change in the producer, or that a change in one (the
cause) is invariably followed by a change in the other (the effect). That
is, one change causes another only if the first can be shown to be either
necessary or *sufficient* for the other. In general it is not easy to establish
either necessity or sufficiency, but difficult or not, it is required before
we can justifiably assume a causal connection.

Science has developed powerful experimental ways of determining
whether variables are causally connected. It is not much of an exag-
geration to say that this is what science is all about. Because of this
capability, science, as noted earlier, is as essential to effective problem
solving as is art. Knowing where, when, and how to use scientific research is part of the art of problem solving. The problem solver who is
not well versed in science can nevertheless demand an explanation in
ordinary English of how proclaimed causal relations were established.
He should require the explanation to be complete enough to enable
him to judge whether a causal claim is based on an association or a
demonstration of either necessity or sufficiency.

The relationship between variables that are causally connected may
not be simple. Under some circumstances, for example, demand may
increase when prices are increased, or it may decrease when prices are
reduced. The effect of price on demand may depend on other variables, for example, competitive pricing. There are products that, like
the Packard automobile, destroyed themselves with reduced pricing.
Those who are addicted to simple relationships tend to dismiss such
examples as "exceptions that prove the rule," whatever that may mean.
Such aberrations, however, can provide valuable clues to more complex and subtle relationships, knowledge of which can yield very creative and effective solutions to problems. Here is a case in point.

Fable 5.5.   THE PRODUCT THAT WANTED
TO BE SECOND BEST.

It is widely assumed that the maximum price people are willing to pay
for a product is affected by the value they impute to it, and there is
plenty of evidence to support this assumption. What is not so apparent

is that the price of a product also affects the value it is believed to have. Price and the perception of value are not independent variables; they interact. The discovery of the nature of this interaction provided an ingenious solution to a marketing problem involving a food product.

The principal product of a food company was the highest priced in its field, but it enjoyed the largest share of its market because it was perceived as a quality product that was "worth the difference." As was to be expected, competitors were devoted to toppling the product from its pinnacle. They tried to do so by decreasing their prices. At first this had no effect, but with continued price reductions by competitors the leading brand began to lose its share of the market. Its producer called in a research group to help find a pricing policy that would protect the product's share of the market with as little loss of profit as possible.

The researchers learned that the price of their sponsor's product had remained constant over many years during which competitive prices had come down. Only after there was a considerable price difference had there been any significant impact on the sales of the sponsor's product. Therefore, the researchers decided to find out how and why the changes in competitive pricing affected the sales of the product they were trying to protect. They looked for a relationship between "how much more the leading product costs than competitive products" and "how much more value consumers believe it to have." They focused their research on the consumers' perceptions of prices and product quality and how these perceptions were related.

First, the researchers took a variety of product types in which there was a large spread of prices among products of the same type. They conducted surveys, asking consumers at what price they believed each brand was currently sold. When the results were plotted, they revealed a curve such as the one shown in Figure 5.1. The prices of products with the lowest prices were underestimated; those with the highest prices were overestimated, and those in the middle were correctly estimated.

Next, the team took classes of products the quality of which could be measured objectively. They measured their quality and then asked consumers to estimate these qualities. The results yielded a curve such as the one shown in Figure 5.2. The estimates of the quality of products with low quality were high, estimates of those with high quality were low, and estimates of those in between were accurate.

From these two sets of observations, the team concluded that the highest priced product in a class would generally be perceived to be higher priced and of lower quality than was actually the case. As the

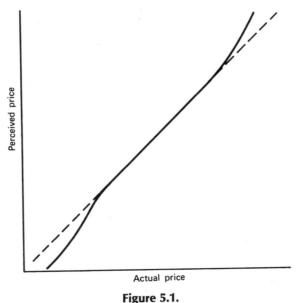

Figure 5.1.

spread of prices between the highest priced product and the next high-est priced increased, the most expensive appeared to increase in rela-tive cost and decrease in relative quality.

A reduction of the price of the sponsor's product would have re-duced its loss of share of market or might possibly have increased it, but this would have required an actual reduction of its quality if its profitability were to be maintained. The company was reluctant to re-duce its product's quality.

Because the research team understood the underlying relationships in this problematic situation, it saw an alternative course of action that otherwise would have been missed. It recommended that the company bring out a significantly higher priced product of even higher quality than its current product. The team argued that this would correct the consumers' perception of the leading brand's price and quality and thus enable it to reclaim its previous share of the market. The company followed this advice, and it worked.

> **MORAL:** **The way variables act may not be nearly as important as how they interact.**

Many effects are the result of interacting causes. We know, for ex-ample, that water boils at a certain temperature but that the boiling

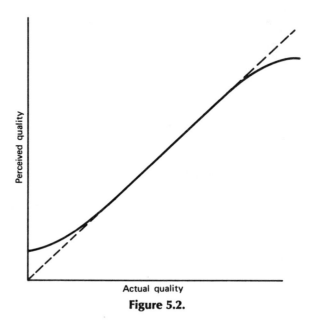

Actual quality

Figure 5.2.

point varies with atmospheric pressure. For this reason it takes longer to prepare a hard-boiled egg in Mexico City than in New York.

Like so many obvious things, the interaction of causal variables is often overlooked. We not only respond to variables in combination, but, even when we respond to only one, we often have a choice as to which to respond to, as the next story shows.

In a conversation about logical thinking among four professors, one asked the others: If two chimney sweeps climbed down a chimney and one came out with a dirty face and the other with a clean face, which one would go to wash his face?

The engineer in the group immediately answered, "The fellow with the dirty face."

The scientist in the group disagreed. He said, "The fellow with the clean face. He would see that the other fellow's face was dirty and would assume his was dirty also, so he would go to wash his face. But the fellow with the dirty face would see that the other's was clean and would assume that his was clean also. So he would not go to wash his face."

The philosopher in the group came to the defense of the engineer. He argued, "When the fellow with the clean face started for the washroom, as the scientist correctly reasoned, the fellow with the dirty face would ask him where he was going. The fellow with the clean face would say, 'To wash my face.' 'Why?' the other would ask, 'your face is clean.' The fellow with the clean face would then say, 'But yours is dirty.' So the fellow with the dirty face would go to wash his face.''

A student who listened to this exchange could contain himself no longer and burst out with the question: "How could two fellows climb down a dirty chimney and one come out with a clean face and the other with a dirty face?''

One can infer different effects from the same cause. Furthermore, one can move from the same cause to the same effect by different routes that are not equally efficient. This is illustrated by the story of a physics professor who asked members of an introductory class how they would determine the height of a tall building using a barometer. One eager science student blurted out that he would measure the atmospheric pressure at ground level and at the top of the building, and convert the difference into the building's height using a well-known physical equation.

A second science student said he would do it differently. He would drop the barometer from the top of the building and measure the length of time it took to reach the ground. Then he would convert this time into the building's height using an equally well-known physical equation.

The professor then asked a shy business administration student how he would do it. The student reluctantly replied that he would give the barometer to the building's chief caretaker and ask him how high the building was.

It is apparent that not all effects are linearly related to their causes; that is, the amount of response is proportional to the amount of stimulus. Few stimuli have responses that are related in this way. Some of a drug may be beneficial, but increases in quantity may not be accompanied by increases in benefit. In fact, as the dosage increases, harmful or lethal effects are possible.

Increases in advertising or sales calls on customers may, after a certain level (the saturation point), fail to yield any additional response from customers. Beyond a still higher level (the supersaturation point) they may produce decreased responses. A study showing that this was the case in one company's advertising is described in detail in Chapter 10.

Now consider the type of relationship that holds between the symptoms of a deficiency and its cause. Symptoms are part of what was previously referred to (in Chapter 4) as facts of the case.

When a patient consults a doctor, he begins by giving him certain facts of his case: symptoms of ill health. Then the doctor usually makes some observations of his own; he takes the patient's temperature, pulse, blood pressure, and so on, and asks additional questions such as: "Does this hurt?" or "Have you been sleeping well?" In this way the doctor finds additional symptoms that are also facts of the case. Once a set of symptoms has been collected, the doctor goes through a *diagnostic* process. In this process he develops a hypothesis or a conclusion about the cause of the deficiency whose symptoms he has observed. Once he is convinced of the validity of the diagnosis—that is, the cause of the illness—he prescribes in a way he believes will remove the cause. If the cause is removed, the symptoms should disappear.

Unfortunately, it does not always work this way. For example, some patients who complain of stomach pains are eventually diagnosed as having duodenal ulcers. One way of treating such ulcers is by surgery that disconnects the duodenum from the stomach. In many cases after such an operation the patient develops a peptic ulcer. Thus the "cause" of an ulcer that was eliminated was not ultimate enough. In some such cases, a doctor prescribes medication that eliminates the patient's stomach pains, thereby removing the symptoms but not the cause. A duodenal ulcer can itself be considered to be a symptom of a psychosomatic disorder.

We have a parallel case in the way alcoholism is treated. It is usually treated as a *problem* to be removed rather than as the alcoholic's *solution* to a serious personal problem. No wonder that when his "solution" is denied him he often returns to it as soon as he can or develops other "solutions" that are equally damaging. The alcoholic's original problem is usually left unsolved when he is denied alcohol or is induced to abstain.

Problem solving is often directed at the removal of symptoms rather than causes. This is particularly true where society is involved. For example, we define *crime* as a social problem, and we attempt to solve it by removing the criminal from society. However, crime continues to rise, and mounting evidence shows that prisons make convicts more likely to commit further crimes when they are released. Thus it is increasingly apparent that crime is a symptom, not a disease, and that we have not been treating its causes adequately. In fact, the treatment is widely recognized as a major cause of the continuing problem.

We tend to look for simple causes of even the most complex problems. This derives to some extent from the success that modern medicine had in its early days with what has come to be known as the "germ theory" of illness. Medical researchers looked for some foreign "bug" that was completely responsible for an ailment and, having found it, tried to remove or suppress it in some way. The success of this approach bred a disposition toward simple causes not only in medicine but in any field in which the subject of study could be thought of as an organism or organism-like.

For example, we consider drug addiction to be a disease caused by drugs. We usually treat it by denying addicts access to the responsible drugs. That we have not succeeded with such treatment is apparent, but our belief in this simple-minded methodology is strong enough to overcome evidence that suggests that another approach is better.

A number of studies have shown that addicts are characteristically disenchanted with and alienated from society. They hold society responsible for their problems and seek to "thumb their noses at it." By making drugs illegal we increase their attractiveness to addicts and others who are alienated from society precisely because the use of something illegal is a way of thumbing one's nose at the society that proscribes its use. Hence our treatment exacerbates the problem; it does not solve it. By legalizing the use of addictive drugs and dispensing them in a controlled way, England has had much more success than America in treating addiction, and it has avoided the huge criminal problem created by the demand for drugs that are illegal.

Most of us think we are immune to such errors, but this is not the case. Much of what we think is problem solving is symptom suppression, and many of the problems we face are the products of solutions we have applied to previous problems.

For example, in systems involving large amounts of similar equipment, regular maintenance is often used to prevent breakdowns. In many such cases maintenance is the principal cause of subsequent breakdowns. This is not unfamiliar to the owners of automobiles who have frequently been victimized by the white-frocked diagnostician in an automotive repair shop. In one study done for a branch of the military, it was found that steam cleaning of motor vehicles was responsible not only for many breakdowns but also for the reduced life of the vehicles. Another study done on railroad locomotives showed that frequent changes of their motor oil accelerated the wear of engines. In this connection "Too much of a good thing is bad" is a useful tautology to keep in mind.

SUMMARY

In attempting to solve a problem we change one or more aspects of the problematic situation with the intention of bringing about a desirable change in some other aspect of it. Whether we succeed depends on the relationship between the aspect that we manipulate and the aspect we want to change. A change in one thing will bring about a change in another only if they are *causally* related.

The fact that two variables are associated—tend to change together in the same or the opposite direction—does not provide an adequate basis for inferring a causal relationship between them. The lack of such co-related changes, however, does provide a basis for inferring the *absence* of a causal relationship under the conditions in which the lack of association was observed. Because of this, the association between variables can be used as a way of selecting those to be studied further for causal connections. Furthermore, the presence of an association between variables enables us to use one of them to predict, but not explain, the other.

A causal relationship between variables cannot be inferred from data *describing* their behavior, but from controlled testing of a causal hypothesis about them. Such hypotheses assert the necessity and/or sufficiency of changes in one for changes in the other.

Causal relationships between variables may be quite complex and may depend on other variables. Such "interactions" may be subtle and difficult to uncover. Experimentation is usually required. One may have to go a long way to gain a little understanding of such relationships, but a little understanding can carry one a long way toward effective solutions of even very complex problems.

Complex problems seldom have simple solutions, that is, solutions that involve manipulating only one causal variable. Deficiencies in societal and organizational performance are seldom due to a single simple foreign element as they sometimes are in biological organisms. The classical disease model is more likely than not to be misleading when applied to organizations.

Finally, to suppress symptoms successfully is not to remove the cause of the deficiency but to invite intensification of the problem whose symptoms are treated. Such treatments often exacerbate the problem in hand and create new and more serious problems.

Science is an almost indispensable aid in establishing causal relationships. Its effective use is a vital part of the art of problem solving.

PART TWO—applications

In Part 1 I resorted to very short fables to illustrate my points. They are, at best, caricatures of reality. They make the creative part of problem solving look either too easy or too mysterious. Creativity is not just a flashing insight. Such insights are nurtured in soil prepared by hard and time-consuming work. To provide a more realistic view of what is involved in creative problem solving, in this part I provide some non-fable-ized illustrations of some of the more important procedures referred to in Part 1.

CHAPTER SIX

The National Scientific Communication and Technology Transfer System: an Idealized Design

To help provide an idea of the content of idealized design and a feeling of the spirit behind it a very brief digest of such a design that is the subject of a recently published book (Ackoff et al., 1976) is provided here. First, some of the background of the design may be helpful.

The large complex of interacting individuals and institutions that are involved in producing, distributing, and marketing scientific and technological information is often referred to as a "system." This complex, however, is clearly not an *organized* system; it is an aggregation of interacting but independently controlled and uncoordinated parts. For convenience I refer to it as the "SCATT System," SCATT being an acronym derived from Scientific Communication and Technology Transfer.

Numerous studies have been directed at improving the efficiency or effectiveness of various parts of this system. Their cumulative effect has not been impressive; they have not produced significant improvements in the system as a whole. Users still complain about the rapidly increasing overload of information, much of which is either redundant or of little value, and about the difficulty and excessive time required to find and acquire at least some of the information they want. Authors, publishers, librarians, and others involved in information services have their own frequently expressed complaints and frustrations. Such dissatisfaction with the current system has led to a large number of changes in its parts, but these have not had a significant overall effect because they, like the system itself, have neither been coordinated nor integrated by the use of any well-defined systemic goals or objectives.

The current system has many virtues: it is far from the worst such system in the world. However, as almost everybody would agree, it is far from the best that is possible. To agree that this is the case is not necessarily to agree on what is the best system possible.

The deficiencies of our current SCATT system are exacerbated by a situation that Dr. Jordan Baruch, a prominent expert in the field, described thus:

> Unlike the fields of physics and chemistry, information science has been deterred in its development by the lack of an appropriate environment in which to perform realistic experiments. . . . In Information science, control has been achieved almost always at the sacrifice of reality while realistic experiments, by and large, had to be conducted in a relatively uncontrolled environment. (From a private communication with permission.)

In 1974–1975 the (then) Office of Science Information Service (now Division of Science Information) of the National Science Foundation sponsored a study at the Busch Center of the Wharton School that was directed at three objectives: to initiate and encourage a massive self-organization effort among the parts of the SCATT System so that their coordination is increased; to engage its participants in defining overall objectives that will unify and improve the net effect of their individual efforts; to provide the information sciences with a much needed laboratory in which significant issues about the system can be resolved.

These objectives were pursued by participative design of an idealized SCATT system. The first version of such a design was produced by a team at the Busch Center. It was widely disseminated for criticism and suggestions, and there was no lack of either. The design was then revised to incorporate as much of the feedback as the team and its advisors believed was relevant and useful. This included most of it. This cycle was continued until most of the changes called for by the feedback were felt to become incremental. Six versions were produced, the last of which was published in the book referred to previously.

Three advisory groups assisted in producing the design: an industrially oriented group, an academically and governmentally oriented group, and a faculty group at the University of Pennsylvania.

As part of the design process, a number of presentations were made to stakeholder groups, members of which were asked to participate and share the fun. Many of them did.

Now to the design itself. Because this is a digest of the design, emphasis is placed on what it does rather than on how it does it.

One general remark about the design may be helpful before describing it: it has a very strong user orientation. This is not to say that it ignores, or is indifferent to, the needs and purposes of other participants in the system; the justification for considering them, however, lies largely in the use that is made of their services and products.

THE DESIGN

Informal communication is generally considered to be the best way to obtain primary or secondary information. The idealized SCATT system is designed to facilitate such communication by supporting existing "invisible colleges," and encouraging the formation of new ones. For example, in the design, members of any group can arrange to receive automatically any information that is judged to be particularly valuable by any other member of the group. No matter how dispersed the members are, they can use the system's terminals to communicate directly with each other, separately or in clusters. They can do so in real time or with delayed response. The system's communication network also enables any reader and any author to communicate with each other.

The system encourages the introduction of young professionals into invisible colleges by providing reduced meeting registration fees to older professionals who bring and sponsor young colleagues and students with them. The younger members can also attend at a reduced fee.

On request, the system can form a list of those of its users who have any specified common interest and inquire of them, before revealing their identity, whether they want to enter the proposed communication that instigated the request. This facilitates the formation of new colleges around new subjects and problems.

The system provides facilities in every part of the country for meetings of any size and duration. These facilities are designed to encourage controlled experimentation on meetings. The system also provides a research and consulting staff that can assist in meeting design, management, and evaluation.

Now consider formal communication in documentary form. The system receives all copyrighted material and approved patents. It also accepts unpublished documents and raw data that have been refereed by an appropriate professional society. There are six requirements for the entry of a document into the system: that it is in machine-readable form with consecutively numbered paragraphs, that it has an index using paragraph designations, that it is preceded by an author-prepared abstract that states what the author thinks is new in his document, that it also has an independently prepared signed abstract arranged for by the publisher if published, that it is appropriately coded in two systems, one using specified categories and the other using weighted key words, finally, that it has been put through a redundancy check.

Redundancy checks are carried out with the assistance of a local SCATT center or an affiliated library. Such checks involve having the classification of the document verified and certified by a center or library, then extracting from the system abstracts of closely related documents. The author's comparison of his submission with these abstracts should be the basis of his statement of what is new in his work. The list of documents checked must be included as part of his submission and may serve readers as a guide to related literature.

Journals publish three types of paper: invited, uninvited but refereed, and a special portion of randomly selected unrefereed papers. This, together with user evaluations to be described in a moment, make it possible to evaluate the editorial practices and quality of refereeing used by a journal. The submission of uninvited papers to journals requires payment of a fee to cover the publisher's services, and a fee is required for the entry of any document into the SCATT system. Authors can submit unpublished documents directly into the system after meeting the pre-entry requirements already referred to. If such a manuscript is subsequently published, it will be withdrawn from the system. Any document in the system can be corrected or otherwise modified by its author for a fee. Authors can also submit "half-baked" ideas, conjectures, or statements of problems deserving attention.

Each professional society is required to publish a periodical that contains brief descriptions of the recent results of research and development and their applications, and to maintain a current record of who is doing what and who is expert on what. Supported by the National Science Foundation (NSF), each society annually appoints a suitable number of Society Fellows who are available for consultation through the system and who prepare annual reviews of the relevant work done outside their fields. In addition, each year the NSF appoints a number of National Fellows who are available for answering inquiries addressed to them through Society Fellows. They prepare annual reviews of their own fields which are translated into various levels of nontechnicality by a stable of science writers maintained by the NSF.

To decrease the volume of unsolicited information that scientists and technologists receive, there is a higher cost for distributing unsolicited documents than solicited ones. For example, fourth-class mail costs more than first-class mail. The system protects the privacy of those who use it.

Each SCATT center maintains meeting-information and technology-exhibit registers. It also maintains a file of all laws, regulations, and ordinances that apply in the area it serves and are relevant to scientists and technologists.

The SCATT system is sensitive and adaptive to the individual needs, levels of sophistication, styles, and idiosyncracies of its users. The software is designed to allow for the varied skills of its users and to be tolerant of errors. The system offers a wide range of services and provides its users with assistance in finding and using relevant ones.

For a fee any individual or institution can use the system's profile-based retrieval service. This service is designed to provide the user with evaluative feedback on his use of it. He can arrange to receive, at a frequency he specifies, a list of all documents, tapes, patents, meetings, or technological exhibits that have entered the system since he received his last listing. Any user of the system can arrange to receive or automatically exclude the output of any person, group, publisher, and so on. He can also arrange to receive automatically any corrections, reviews, commentaries, or primary messages based on a specified document.

The profile-based retrieval system can also be used on a "one-shot" basis. Groups of individuals or institutions may use a common profile and thereby reduce the cost of the service. Every user is free to design and use his own retrieval system or to employ any one of a number of standard procedures that are made available to him by the system. The system thereby learns of needs that are not being met and of better ways to serve needs that have already been identified.

The normal retrieval process involves three phases: first, the provision of a list of documents; second, the provision of secondary information about documents for which it is requested; and third, the provision of the documents themselves, or specified parts of, or passages from, them. The user is free to skip any of these phases if he wants to.

Listings of documents that have been in the system for more than a year include summary information on their quality ratings provided by previous users. Beside each item on lists prepared by the system, the user is asked to indicate whether he found it "not relevant," "relevant but don't want," or "want." For all secondary information he receives, he is asked to indicate whether it is "not relevant," "relevant but not useful," or "relevant and useful." For each document he receives, he is asked to indicate its relevance and usefulness and, in addition, whether he considers it to be of high, medium, or low quality. This information is used to improve the classification and retrieval system, to suggest to users how their profiles may be improved, and to provide feedback to publishers and authors on users' evaluations of their documents.

Users can obtain documents or tapes from local SCATT centers or from affiliated libraries. Publishers provide each center with machine-readable or reproducible master copies of their publications. When these are reproduced for a user by a center or an affiliated library, a fee is charged, part of which goes to the publisher and part to the center or library. Local SCATT centers maintain a register of libraries in their areas at which hard copies of documents registered in the system can be obtained. Journals and books are available for purchase either from their publishers or through the system. The subscription cost of journals published by professional societies is separated from dues so that members are free *not* to subscribe to them. This is intended to reduce the number and size of low-quality journals and the amount of useless information imposed on users.

As the description of the idealized SCATT system indicates, all the system's services are charged for. The free-market mechanism is used to facilitate individual and collective evaluation of services by users. This arrangement encourages competition and the creation of new services, particularly where demand is not well served by the system. The system itself would maintain a research and development unit responsible for the design and implementation of new services.

The system consists of a national SCATT center, about a dozen regional SCATT centers, and between 100 and 150 local SCATT centers. The number of affiliated libraries is unlimited. Once set up, the system is required to be self-supporting. It is not to be allowed to receive operating subsidies from any source. External support of its operations can only take the form of subsidies made available to its users. Charges made by the system take into account the user's ability to pay and his need for the particular service requested. Subsidies to users may well be administered by libraries.

There is profit-and-loss accounting for each SCATT center, whether national, regional, or local. Local SCATT centers, but not national or regional centers, can be privately owned and operated for a profit. They can be placed in or attached to existing libraries, mainly large public or university libraries.

There is participative management by all users at all levels of the SCATT organization. Stakeholders are encouraged to identify needs that are not being met, to provide feedback on existing services, and to join in making decisions that affect them.

Since the publication of the complete idealized design, a number of different significant components of the SCATT system have begun to collaborate with the Wharton Group under NSF sponsorship. These efforts are directed toward designing, implementing, and evaluating changes in these subsystems that are compatible with the overall design. This overall design has become the focus of continuing discussion that offers hope of leading to more intensive and extensive collaboration between parts of the system. In Mexico the government launched a companion project that produced a compatible idealized design, implementation of which has been initiated. At this writing there is talk of similar efforts in several other countries.

CHAPTER SEVEN

Transportation Without A Future:
A Reference Projection*

This chapter provides a detailed example of a reference projection. Urban transportation in the United States is projected to the year 2000.

Recall that a reference projection is an extrapolation from the past into the future assuming that the system involved and its environment will develop without intervention, that is, with no change of the trends experienced over the relevant past. Recall also that such a projection is not a forecast of what will happen but of what *would* happen if there were no interventions. Since some interventions are very likely, a reference projection is more a forecast of what is *not* likely to happen than of what will.

The purpose of a reference projection is to identify when and how a system will break down if there are no interventions. By so doing, one can plan interventions *now* rather than wait, as it usually the case, until the system is in a state of crisis. Interventions under crisis conditions seldom provide effective solutions to problems. Planned interventions are more likely to be creative and effective.

Moreover, reference projections can be used to suggest creative types of intervention, ones that would not normally be considered even in planning prior to a state of crisis. This chapter also provides an example of such solution-generation.

The automobile currently accounts for about eighty-five percent of all urban passenger travel. This percentage has been increasing and will continue to increase unless restrictions are introduced deliberately

* This case is extracted from Sagasti and Ackoff (1971).

Table 7.1.   Projected Population Growth

Year	Population (in millions)	Percentage over 20
1960	180.6	61.0
1970	206.0	60.9
1980	239.3	61.5
1990	288.6	60.9
2000	321.9	62.4

Source: Landsberg et al., 1963, Table A.1.3.

or are self-generated because of increases in (1) our adult population, (2) the number of automobiles per adult, and (3) the miles per year that vehicles are driven.

The projected growth of our total and adult (over 20 years) population is shown in Table 7.1.

The projected number of automobiles per adult is shown in Table 7.2. These projections assume continued expansion of city streets and highways at a rate that will not reduce recent trends of increasing usage of automobiles; that is, they assume unconstrained growth. They also assume that a "saturation point" is not reached with respect to the number of automobiles per adult.

In what follows we do not use the high projection for the number of automobiles per adult, because it appears to go beyond the saturation point. Bottiny (1966) suggested that a reasonable saturation point for automobile ownership is one automobile per licensed operator. It is difficult to imagine 1.51 automobiles per adult in the year 2000.

To estimate the future unconstrained volume of automobile traffic, it is also necessary to estimate the average miles per vehicle per year.

Table 7.2.   Projected Number of Automobiles per Adult

Year	Low	Medium	High
1960	0.54	0.54	0.54
1980	0.76	0.79	0.91
2000	1.06	1.19	1.51

Source: Landsberg et al., 1963, Tables A.5.1 and A.5.2.

Table 7.3.   Average Miles per Vehicle per Year

Year	Automobiles	All Passenger Vehicles[a]	Trucks and Trailers	All Vehicles
1950	9020	9078	10,776	9369
1955	9359	9400	10,697	9615
1960	9446	9474	10,585	9652
1965	9255	9278	11,373	9674

Source: Bureau of Public Roads, 1967, Table VM-201A.
[a] Includes buses and automobiles.

Data on past usage are shown in Table 7.3 which also includes data on vehicles other than automobiles.

According to Lansing and Hendricks (1967):

The relation between family income and thousands of miles travelled is surprisingly close to a straight line. . . . It may be a good approximation to say that every dollar of additional income leads to one additional mile of travel.

As people's income rises, the number of vehicle-miles which they travel may be expected to rise in proportion. . . . Over a period of 10, 20, 30 years one should project an increase in average vehicle miles at approximately the same rate as average stability of the relation between income and mileage (p. 23).

Lansing and Hendricks (1967) also showed that the average automobile usage per year is higher for those who live in metropolitan areas than for the population as a whole. However, their result, 13,000 miles *per family* in metropolitan areas, is not directly comparable with the *per vehicle* data of Table 7.3. They also observed that the average number of miles travelled by suburbanites (14,000 miles per family) is substantially higher than that of urbanites (less than 9000 miles per family).

Unfortunately it is not possible to combine the historical data of Table 7.3 with that obtained by Lansing and Hendricks to obtain a precise projection of the average miles per automobile per year. Nevertheless it is possible to use the data they provided in a qualitative way together with expected rises in income and shifts to suburbs and conclude that the average miles per automobile per year will continue to increase slowly under the assumption of unconstrained growth.

Table 7.4.   Percentage of Total Increase in Population
in the U.S.A.

Area	1950–1960	1960–1966
SMSAs		
Central Cities	22	9
Fringe	66	75
Outside SMSA	12	16
Total U.S.A.	100	100

Source: Department of Housing and Urban Transportation (1968a).

Landsberg et al. (1963) estimated that the disposable income per
household will increase from about $6500 in the early 1960s to nearly
$10,000 in 1980 and somewhere between $13,000 and $15,000 by the
end of the century (p. 8). In addition to this, the trend toward increasing suburbanization is indicated by the relative growth of central cities
and fringe areas within a Standard Metropolitan Statistical Area (SMSA).
As seen in Table 7.4, it is in the urban fringe that the largest percentage
increase of population is occurring.

These two factors, increase of family income and suburbanization,
combined with the results obtained by Lansing and Hendricks, point
in the direction of an increase in the average miles travelled by a family per year. Part of this increase will be due to increasing automobile
ownership and part due to extended usage of the automobile. Following the policy of favoring the existing system, we take into consideration only the historical growth and extrapolate it into the future, keeping in mind that further increases in the average miles per automobile
per year are not only possible but likely. Table 7.5 gives the constrained
growth in average miles per automobile per year, based on the average
growth over the period from 1950 to 1965.

Using the information contained in Tables 7.1 to 7.5, estimates of
the total number of automobiles and vehicle miles can be prepared
using the 59.49 million automobiles of 1960 as a base. This is done as
follows:

(Population over 20) $\times$ (Automobiles/adult) = Total number of
automobiles

(Total number of automobiles) $\times$ (Average miles per automobile) =
Total vehicle miles

Table 7.5.   Projected Average Miles per Automobile per Year[a]

Year	Miles per Automobile per Year
1960	9,446
1980	9,759
2000	10,072

[a] Calculated from Table 7.4 by taking the average growth rate every five years from 1950 to 1965 and extrapolating to 1980 and 2000.

The results of such calculations for each of the two growth rates of number of automobiles per adult are shown in Table 7.6.

During the past fifteen years approximately fifty percent of the miles travelled in a given year was in urban areas, as indicated in Table 7.7. Using different projection methods, Wilbur Smith and Associates (1966, p. 36) estimated that by 1980 about sixty percent of the total vehicle miles travelled will be on urban roads and that by 2000 this will increase to about sixty-five percent. Table 7.7 shows that the historical percentage distribution of urban-rural miles for automobiles and all vehicles has remained practically constant at about fifty percent for the past two decades.

Continuing our policy of being conservative, we assume that urban vehicle miles will account for fifty percent of the automobile vehicle miles in 1980 and 2000 even though the estimates made by Wilbur Smith and Associates are significantly higher.

By applying these percentages to the data shown in Table 7.6 we can estimate unconstrained total *urban* automobile miles per year. The results are shown in Table 7.8.

Table 7.6.   Projections of Total Automobile Miles (in Millions) for Various Growth Rates in Automobiles per Adult Year

Year	Low	Medium
1960	561,943	561,943
1980	1,091,544	1,134,581
2000	2,144,453	2,407,510

Table 7.7.   Percentage Distribution for Urban-Rural Miles Travelled[a]

Year	Automobiles		All Vehicles[b]	
	Urban	Rural	Urban	Rural
1950	50.2	49.8	47.6	52.4
1955	47.4	52.6	45.4	54.6
1960	48.4	51.6	46.1	53.9
1965	50.3	49.7	47.8	52.2

[a] Estimated from Table VM-201, Bureau of Public Roads (1967).
[b] Includes automobiles, buses, and trucks.

Thus far we have considered unconstrained growth in traffic volume due to automobile travel, but buses and trucks will also generate their share of traffic volume.

Projections of urban truck traffic are only available in specific studies of cities, and these vary in the amount of detail they provide. The data from different sources are difficult to combine with the aggregated statistics provided by government agencies. Table 7.9 shows historical data and extrapolations to 1975 on the vehicle miles travelled by buses and trucks and their relation to automobile vehicle miles.

Table 7.9 shows that the volume of traffic generated by buses can be neglected without introducing substantial error and that the ratio of truck vehicle miles to automobile vehicle miles has remained, and is expected to remain, stable at a value between one-fourth and one-fifth. Therefore, when analyzing increases in traffic volume—the ratio of projected vehicle miles in 1980 and 2000 to vehicle miles in 1960—it is

Table 7.8.   Urban Automobile Miles per Year (in Millions) for Various Ownership Growth Rates

Year	Low		Medium	
	Miles	Percentage of 1960	Miles	Percentage of 1960
1960	280,972	100.0	280,972	100.0
1980	545,772	194.2	567,291	201.9
2000	1,072,226	381.6	1,203,755	428.4

Table 7.9. Past and Extrapolated Vehicle Miles (in Millions) for Buses and Trucks and Ratios to Automobile Vehicle Miles

Year	Trucks Vehicle Miles	Trucks Ratio to Automobile	Buses Vehicle Miles	Buses Ratio to Automobile	Automobiles Vehicle Miles
1950	90,552	0.25	4081	0.01	363,613
1955	108,817	0.22	4194	0.008	492,635
1960	126,409	0.21	4353	0.007	588,083[a]
1965	173,659	0.24	4684	0.007	709,800
1970	209,200	0.24	4760	0.005	891,800
1975	249,000	0.23	4890	0.005	1,084,000

Sources: Department of Housing and Urban Development (1968a) and Bureau of Public Roads (1967).
[a] This figure differs from that given in Table 7.6 by 4.5 percent due to differences in the method of calculation.

enough to take into consideration the volume of traffic (vehicle miles) generated by automobiles.

Now to the question: How many additional miles of urban highways would be required to maintain the 1960 level of congestion? To answer this question we use information made available by the National Academy of Sciences (1960). The data apply to 1958, but little error results from using them for 1960. The measures used were explained thus:

> In an overall consideration of the problem of road utilization, it is the latter group of highways [major roads] that is approaching capacity. Since the Federal-aid primary highway system roughly approximates the roads most intensively used, a comparison was made of its actual usage and its capacity.
>
> In order to estimate the degree of utilization of the Federal-aid primary system it was necessary to calculate the *practical* and the *possible* capacities of the system. Practical capacity represents the maximum number of vehicles that can pass a given point in one hour *under prevailing conditions, without unreasonable delay or restrictions to the driver's freedom to maneuver.* Possible capacity, on the other hand, represents the maximum number of vehicles that can pass a given point on a lane or roadway during one hour under the prevailing roadway and traffic conditions (p. 76, italics ours).

Table 7.10 gives the results obtained.

Table 7.10. Relation Between Highway Usage and Capacity of the Federal-Aid Primary System

	Rural	Urban	Total
Extent of system (miles)	261,791	20,076	286,867
Average daily traffic (million vehicle miles)			
Actual usage	571	257	828
Practical capacity	897	284	1,181
Possible capacity	2,460	443	2,903
Ratio of capacity to usage			
Practical capacity	1.57	1.10	1.43
Possible capacity	4.31	1.72	3.51
Proportion of capacity used (%)			
Practical capacity	64	90	70
Possible capacity	23	58	29

Source: Reprinted from *U.S. Transportation: Resources Performance, and Problems,* page |77, with the permission of the National Academy of Sciences, Washington, D.C.

The National Academy noted, "The urban portions of the Federal-aid primary system are operating at 90 percent of their practical capacity. . . . The margin is uncomfortably thin" (p. 77).

If urban traffic congestion is to be maintained at the 1958 level and no major shifts in traffic from the Federal-aid highway system to other systems ocur, we can estimate the additional highway miles (assuming a standard four-lane highway) in the Federal-aid system as follows. Using the low growth rate of automobiles per adult, for example, there will be about 3.82 times as many urban automobile miles in 2000 as in 1960. We will need about this many more urban highway miles in the Federal-aid primary system to retain the 1958 level of congestion; that is,

$$3.82 \times 20,076 \text{ miles} = 76,690 \text{ miles}.$$

There were 20,076 miles in this system in 1960.

Table 7.11 shows the miles required in 1980 and 2000 for low and medium growth of automobile ownership.

The Federal-aid system consists of the major roads that are used for the movement of people and goods *through* an area, as contrasted with

Table 7.11. Estimated Miles of Standard Urban Highway Required in the Federal-Aid Primary System to Maintain 1960 Level of Congestion

| | Growth Rate | |
Year	Low	Medium
1980	38,987	40,533
2000	76,690	86,006

movements having origin or destination *within* one area. These are the roads that carry a heavy traffic load and provide access to residential locations, to the central business district, to industrial areas, to peripheral business areas, and so on, that is, to the main destinations in urban areas. When traffic congestion increases in this system, it also increases on other urban streets and highways not included in the system. For this reason a major shift of urban traffic from the Federal-aid primary system to other urban roads is not expected.

Using the low growth rate of automobile ownership, about 55,000 (76,690–20,076) additional miles of urban highways will be required in year 2000 to maintain the 1960 level of congestion. At the *very conservative* estimate of an average cost of $10 million per mile of standard four-lane urban highway (Lyle Fitch and Associates, 1964, p. 14), the total investment required over the next thirty years would be approximately $550 billion, or an average of $18.3 billion per year. This constitutes more than a threefold increase in the *total* expenditure for transportation facilities in 1967 (approximately $5.35 billion). The amount required ($18.3 billion) is more than *ten times* the amount spent on urban highways in 1967 ($1.4 billion). Such an increase in expenditure is virtually impossible, but it is not the only obstacle to constrained growth of automobile usage.

The amount of land that can be allocated to roads, highways, and parking spaces in urban areas, particularly in the central business district, also limits such growth. Lyle Fitch and Associates (1964) quote Senator Harrison Williams on this subject:

Even if we were to try [to solve urban transportation problems by highways alone] with an urban highway program averaging $10 to $20 million a mile in high density urban areas, there is every possibility that the remedy would only succeed in killing the patient—

Table 7.12. Proportion of Central Business District Land Devoted to Streets and Parking

CBD	Year	Streets	Parking	Streets and Parking
		Percentage of CBD Devoted to		
Los Angeles	1960	35.0	24.0	59.0
Chicago	1956	31.0	9.7	40.7
Detroit	1953	38.5	11.0	49.5
Minneapolis	1958	34.6	13.7	48.3
Dallas	1961	28.5	12.9	41.4

Source: Wilbur Smith and Associates (1966, Table 11, p. 59).

by replacing valuable tax ratable property with nontaxable concrete and asphalt, by creating huge downtown parking demands which would further remove land for commercial and cultural purposes, and by slowly carving away the activities that created the demand for access in the first place (p. 14).

In most cities the proportion of land devoted to streets and parking in downtown areas already exceeds 40% of the total land available. Table 7.12 shows the relevant percentages for five metropolitan areas.

Clearly, these percentages cannot be increased 3.82 times. Many cities, of course, have smaller percentages, and additional highways (for example, ones bypassing the CBD) need not generate additional parking requirements. Nevertheless it is clear that the space constraint would be reached for increases less than twice the current allocations.

Proposals have been made to use two-level highways to avoid the space problem. The costs associated with this are much higher than those for surface-level highways. Thus, if construction of the "required" conventional road is economically infeasible, as we have demonstrated, building elevated highways would be even less feasible.

Therefore, it does not appear to be practical to expand the existing urban road and highway system to cope with the unconstrained growth of traffic volume over the next thirty years because of the expenditures of money and amounts of space such expansion would require.

We have not considered such social costs as might arise from increased accident rates, increased air pollution, and decreased attractiveness of the environment. The consideration of these costs would provide additional support to the conclusion that we will not be able to solve the urban transportation problem by expanding the highway and road system.

(The study of which the reference projection presented above in part went on to consider other changes in the city that might reduce the projected requirement for highways. It showed that these cannot be expected to significantly affect the requirements. It also showed that it is unlikely that mass transit and highway and vehicle technology now under development will significantly reduce this requirement. The study did find several possible directions in which possible solutions might be found. I include only one of these here. It is sufficient to show how reference projections can be used to reveal both the nature of a future problem and creative solutions to it.)

There are no signs that increasing reliance on the automobile will be affected by increasing traffic congestion or the inconveniences derived from the widespread use of the automobile. On the contrary, there is some evidence that urbanites would prefer to relocate their jobs or residences rather than switch from the automobile to another mode of transportation. The Department of Housing and Urban Transportation (1968b) noted that:

> The experience of recent years contradicts the belief that traffic congestion will set itself a limit to car ownership. If there is to be any chance of coexisting with the automobile in the urban environment, *a different sort of automobile is needed* with improvements in the supporting systems (p. 41, italics ours).

The present design of the automobile, the five to six passenger family car, is a compromise intended to satisfy a wide variety of needs. Automobiles are used for inter- and intracity travel, to and from work, recreation, shopping, and so on.

Of considerable importance is the fact that the number of two-car families increased from seven percent in 1950 to twenty-five percent in 1966. This and other facts we consider later suggest a functional differentiation between an intra- and intercity automobile. Families that own or use more than one car would obtain distinct advantages by using special-purpose automobiles better suited for specific needs, for example, cars better suited to the characteristics of center-city traffic.

A major improvement in automotive systems is suggested by the figures on automobile occupancy in urban areas. For example, average occupancy rates in metropolitan Philadelphia are approximately 1.5 passengers per car, ranging from 1.2 for commuting trips to 1.6 for nonwork trips (*Penn-Jersey Transportation Study,* 1964, p. 91). The average capacity of an automobile, on the other hand, is about five

people. It is apparent that substantial reduction in automobile congestion could be obtained if the average occupancy of automobiles, particularly for work trips, were increased. Car pooling, however, reduces
the advantages of door-to-door travel by automobile. A less incon-
veniencing alternative would involve the use of small urban automobiles, what have been referred to by some as "urmobiles."

This alternative has been explored in several studies (for example,
Cars for Cities and Department of Housing and Urban Development,
1968b). It is generally acknowledged, however, that at higher speeds
and in free-flowing traffic the effect of reduced vehicle length on congestion is very small. For example, at forty miles per hour the majority
of the road space can be said to be occupied by safety space between
vehicles, and, according to McClenehan and Simkowitz (1969) the effect of reducing car length by half on expressway traffic would be an
increase in flow of no more than ten to fifteen percent. Greater increases would occur on heavily used city streets; as much as a seventy
percent increase in flow would be achived when congestion reached
the not-uncommon level of fifteen vehicles per light. If only a fraction
of long cars is replaced by small ones, the resulting flow is approximately a linear interpolation between the two extremes.

Relatively little is known about the effect of car width on traffic flow.
Experiments carried out by the Ministry of Transport in England (*Cars
for Cities*, p. 13) showed that a lane width two and one-half to three
feet wider than the car itself represents a reasonable minimum for
safety purposes. They also showed that in mixed traffic conditions,
when small and large cars travel together, the small ones usually travel
behind the larger ones using the same road space.

A considerable increase in passenger density could be obtained by
the use of short (less than ten feet) and narrow (three and one-half feet)
two-passenger vehicles, one passenger seated behind the other. If traffic were made up exclusively of such vehicles, an increase of at least
2.2 (2.0 × 1.1*) on expressways (two vehicles per normal lane and a
ten percent increase in flow due to shorter cars) and 3.4 (2.0 × 1.7*) on
city streets could be obtained. If shoulders of four-lane expressways
were used for one lane of such vehicles, their capacity would increase
by 2.7 (2.2 + 0.5), and the additional lane would be used for one narrow car which would have half the width of a normal car. Following a
similar line of reasoning, city streets with two moving lanes for current
automobiles and one for parking, the increase would be 5.1 (3.4 + 1.7).
These calculations do not take trucks and buses into account, but they

* Using McClenehan and Simkowitz figures for the increase in traffic flow with short
cars.

show it is possible to deal even with the 4.28 medium forecasted increase in requirements for the year 2000 if the small car we have described were generally adopted.

Parking requirements would also be greatly reduced. For example, a normal car takes more than twenty feet along the sidewalks. Three ten-foot-long cars could be parked in the linear space required for two normal cars, and additional road space would be left free for vehicular traffic. Parking space requirements could be further reduced if the door or doors were either sliding on the side or placed at the front or back. The latter would permit face-in parking with very high density.

A large variety of small automobiles is under development now (*Mechanics Illustrated*, October 1969, p. 76 and *Life*, December 11, 1970). In many cases the new designs incorporate changes that will reduce the polluting effects of cars, and, because of their decreased weight and lower speeds, they would greatly reduce fuel consumption. They can be made to hook on to each other in train-like fashion to facilitate towing or taking the family along on a trip (using nonmotorized cabs, for example). Their reduced maximum speed and acceleration capabilities increase their safety.

The advantages of using small cars for intracity traffic depend on the restrictions imposed on the use of large vehicles. During a transitional period, vehicles of different sizes can mix together. Eventually the use of city streets and highways could be limited to small cars from, say, 7:00 a.m. to 7:00 p.m. on week days. In some cities trucks are already kept off CBD streets during these hours.

Many benefits could derive from publicly or privately owned fleets of small cars that would be available as drive-it-yourself taxis. Their pick-up and drop-off points could be widely dispersed over the city (see *Minicar Transit System*).

It is clear that a change to small urban automobiles can be accomplished in at least a decade. Furthermore, such a change would require little public cost and would yield economies to the individual without the loss of convenience or comfort. Most important, it could reduce congestion significantly and permit less restricted use of automobiles than would otherwise be possible.

CHAPTER EIGHT

A Multidimensional
Organizational Structure[*]

In Chapter 3 it was pointed out that the conventional way of graphically representing organizational structure in two-dimensional trees constrained the numbers and kinds of alternative designs that we normally consider. The design that is presented in this chapter is intended to show how the concept of organizational structure opens up when we remove this representational constraint. Such removal of constraints is necessary if we are to deal effectively with the accelerating rate of technological and social change.

It is apparent that the rates of technological and social change are increasing. Alvin Toffler (1971), among others, has argued that our inability to cope with such acceleration, an inability he calls "Future Shock," is the principal producer of many of the social, institutional, and organizational crises that confront us. Although those who point out the crises do so in harmony, there is considerable discord among them when they come to suggesting cures. It is not surprising, therefore, that enterprises, institutions, and societies continue to be managed and organized much as they were before the awareness of their bombardment by change was widespread.

Most institutions and enterprises seek what Donald Schon (1971) called a "stable state." Their resistance to change tends to be proportional to the need for it. The more turbulent their environment, the more stable the equilibrium they seek. They fail to realize that the only equilibrium that can be obtained in a turbulent environment—like that

[*] Adapted from Ackoff (1977).

obtained by a ship in a rough sea—is dynamic. A turbulent environment requires that institutions be ready, willing, and able to change themselves. Without changing themselves, they cannot adapt effectively to external change.

How can organizations be designed to be more *flexible* and therefore more capable of being changed and changing themselves? Flexibility does not guarantee adaptability, but it is essential for it.

The design of a flexible, or any other kind, of organizational structure is part of what some call "social architecture." In architectural terms what is presented here is a sketch rather than a working drawing. It is a presentation of an idea, a theme, on which a number of variations can be written. (See for example, Goggin, 1974.)

INPUTS AND OUTPUTS

Organizations are purposeful systems some of whose parts are purposeful individuals among whom there is a functional division of labor. Their purposefulness entails choice of *ends* (desired outcomes: objectives and goals) and *means* (courses of action). Courses of action necessarily involve the use of resources (inputs) to produce goods or services (outputs) that are intended to be of greater value to those who consume them than are the inputs. The resources consumed include manpower, materials and energy, plant and equipment, and/or money. This is as true of organizations that are nonprofit as for those that are for profit, and as true for those that are publicly owned as for those that are privately owned.

Traditionally, organizational structure is taken to deal with two types of relationship: (1) *responsibility,* who is responsible for what and (2) *authority,* who reports to whom. Structure so conceived lends itself to representation by a two-dimensional tree in which boxes represent responsibilities and altitude and lines represent the loci and flow of authority.

The conventional representation of an organization's structure does not show either what inputs flow into what outputs or what means are used for what ends. An input-output matrix is seldom used to describe an organization's structure; a means-ends matrix virtually never is. However, these matrices can reveal new and more flexible ways of structuring organizations. In developing this point I use for illustration a typical privately owned corporation engaged in producing goods. Other types of organization, public and private, are used in subsequent illustrations.

An organization's outputs can be used to define its ends, for example, outputs classified by product type or brands. An organizational unit whose responsibility is to provide a product or service to consumers outside the organization is referred to as a *program,* and such units are represented by $P_1, P_2, \ldots, P_k$.

Activities are the means employed by programs. They can usually be divided into *operations,* activities that directly affect the nature or availability of the company's output, and *services,* activities that are required to support programs or operations. Typical operations ($O_1, O_2, \ldots, O_m$) are raw material purchasing, transportation, production, distribution, and marketing. Typical services ($S_1, S_2, \ldots, S_n$) are provided by accounting, data processing, maintenance, industrial relations, finance, personnel, and legal units.

A precise and completely general distinction between operations and services is difficult to make, but doing so is not essential to the concept of organizational structure developed here.

The way activities feed into programs and into activities themselves can be displayed in such tables as those shown in Figures 8.1 and 8.2. The output of each activity may be consumed by programs and other activities, additionally by the executive function (discussed below), by

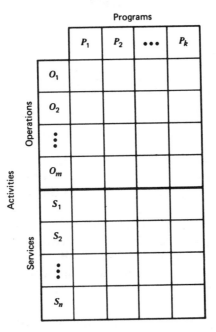

Figure 8.1.

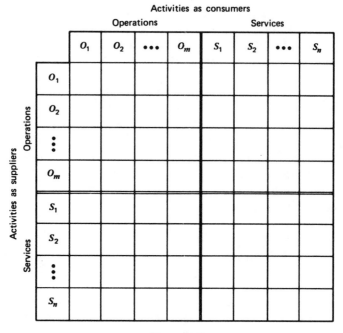

Figure 8.2.

external consumers (also discussed below), and by that activity itself—for example, an accounting unit may prepare its own accounts.

Programs can be divided into subprograms which are defined, for example, by type of customer (industrial or individual), geographic region supplied or serviced, brands, and so on. Subprograms can also be subdivided.

Activities can be similarly divided. For example, a manufacturing operation may be divided into parts production, subassembly, and assembly, and each of these may be subdivided further. The same is true for service units. For example, a financial department can be divided into payroll, accounts receivable, accounts payable, and so on.

If the number of programs plus line and support activities (operations and services) exceeds the number an executive can reasonably coordinate, coordinators may be required within the executive function (see Figure 8.3). More than one coordinator or coordinating unit may be required on any one dimension. If the number of coordinators justify it, supracoordinators or coordinating units may be required. It should be emphasized that in this context "coordination" means *coordination*, not *direction*. Coordination may well be provided by a group made up of the heads of the coordinated units and the executive.

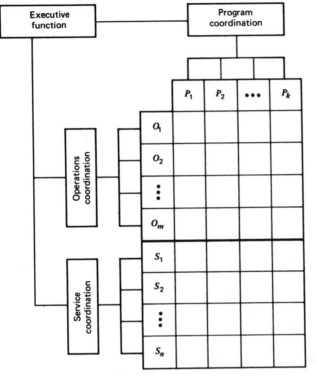

Figure 8.3.

Now consider how a multidimensional (MD) organization can be operated to maximize its flexibility and responsiveness to changing internal and external conditions.

PROGRAMS

1. Programs should be formulated so that they require more than one source of input. These sources may be internal or external. A program that requires only one such source should be combined with another to meet this condition. As will be seen, the more activities a program requires, the more flexibility it can be managed. The corresponding requirement should be imposed on activities. They should be designed to be useful by more than one program and, in the case of services, by more than one line activity.

2. The objective of each program should be defined so that the benefits that can be derived from it can be measured. Further, be-

cause its costs can be measured, a specified function of its benefits and costs, such as profit, can and should be used to measure its performance.

3. Programs should be provided with managers and their personal staffs, *but no other personnel.* They should not be organizational units in the usual sense. They should be managements whose function is to specify, acquire, coordinate, and control such input activities of others as are required to attain their objectives. They should have no authority over those who supply these services, but they should be able to control them in a way revealed in paragraph 6.

4. Programs should *not* be provided with plant or equipment. They should involve no investment.

5. Programs require and should be provided with operating capital. They should receive at least as much of the income they generate as required to cover their operating costs. If they do not generate sufficient capital for this purpose, they can either borrow money to be paid back subsequently or be subsidized. They should be subsidized only when their actual or expected benefits exceed their costs and their costs exceed their income.

6. Programs can buy goods and services from either internal activity units or external suppliers *as they see fit.* It is through their purchasing power that they control and coordinate their suppliers. For practical reasons it may be necessary to constrain this freedom of choice, for example, because proprietary information is involved. The formulation or technology of a product, or its production processes, may be "classified" information; hence the company may be unwilling to have it produced externally. Wherever such a constraint is imposed on a program by the executive function, the saving, if any, that could be obtained by breaking the constraint should be determined. This should be paid to the program by the executive function. If the constraint is self-imposed by the program, there should be no such payment. It is possible, of course, that there is no suitable external source, leaving the program no choice.

These conditions ensure ease of evaluating and comparing program performance and thus make it possible to allocate resources in a way that reflects both their productivity and their relative importance to the organization as a whole. This is as true in nonprofit organizations as it is in ones for profit and private organizations.

Programs are ends-oriented units. Their managers should be concerned exclusively with the attainment of the objectives that define them, not with providing the means required for their pursuit. Unless constrained by the executive function, they can buy these either from within or without, wherever they can obtain the best buy. They pay for services obtained from within just as they do for those obtained from without. This means that internal suppliers must compete with external suppliers for the "businesss" of the programs.

Because programs require no investment and only a few people, they can easily be added, subtracted, or otherwise modified. This gives the organization great flexibility.

The performance measures applied to subprograms can and should be constructed so that their sum is equal to the measure of performance applied to the programs of which they are parts. Program directors can allocate their operating capital to subprograms just as the executive or program coordinator does to programs.

Programs are what might be called the "leading edge" of the MD organization. They are what organizations are about. All other organizational activities are justified primarily in terms of their contributions to programs.

ACTIVITY UNITS

1. Activity units are provided with personnel, plant, and equipment as required. These are treated as investments that are expected to provide the organization with an adequate return.

2. They can sell their goods and/or services to programs and/or external customers as they see fit unless explicitly constrained from, and compensated for not, doing so by the executive function. Therefore, they operate much as independent enterprises, whether their parent organization is publicly or privately owned.

3. These units receive no subsidies, only investments. They are expected to generate their own operating capital from the sale of their output. They can borrow money internally or externally but are expected to pay back such loans. If they are not self-supporting, the parent organization may either allow them to go out of business, sell them, or take them over and reorganize them.

As previously indicated, if the parent organization wants an activity unit to withhold its products or services from external customers, it should pay the unit for doing so. The amount involved should be at least as great as the profits that the unit would have made from the curtailed sales of its output. This makes it possible to account for means and ends separately and to focus each director's attention on a well-defined responsibility. It also makes it possible to put financial responsibility for executive decisions on the executive function and to account for it meaningfully. The executive function can receive a return on its investment and loans, share unit profits, and incur costs.

Activity units and programs turn over a portion of their profits to the parent organization, but they should be allowed to retain some for self-determined reinvestment or other appropriate self-development activities.

Programs and activity units are virtually autonomous. As long as they perform satisfactorily, there is no need for intervention from above. The same is true for subprograms and subactivities.

If the executive observes that a service or product not provided internally is consumed heavily within the organization, he may add an appropriate activity unit or extend an existing one. Any existing activity unit may do the same on its own initiative if it can do so without subsidy.

If an activity unit is used heavily by external but not internal consumers, the executive should want to know why. Either the programs are not purchasing wisely or they no longer need the goods or services provided by the activity unit. In the latter case the activity unit may either be converted into a program, be sold, or be discontinued. On the other hand, if an activity unit has little or no external sales and it has a capacity to meet an external demand that can be shown to exist, the executive should also want to know why. Chances are that it is not being managed competitively.

If an activity unit is used heavily by external consumers, the executive function may well decide to create a program defined by that unit's output. For example, if an internal data-processing unit develops a large external business, the executive function may decide to put the organization as a whole into this business by creating a data-processing program. Unless constrained from doing so by the executive function, the data-processing activity unit would continue to service external customers and the program might use this unit's services.

Activity units can also have an MD organizational design. For example, a research and development unit, as well as an independent company of this type, can set up its projects as programs. Its operating units could consist of disciplinary groups, for example, mathematics, physics, and so on. Its services could consist of such things as drafting, computation, editing, duplicating, and so on. Because any part of an organization can have an MD design, the whole need not be so designed. This makes it possible to convert a traditional organization to the MD type in stages, starting at the bottom, the top, or somewhere in between.

Activity units can sell their services to other activity units as well as to programs and to the executive function as well. For example, an accounting or personnel unit may be used by every other unit of the organization. On the other hand, an accounting or personnel unit may use the marketing unit to sell its services externally.

As previously noted, programs and activity units can be subdivided using product classes, types of customer, geographic regions, and so on. Where consumers of program outputs are numerous and widely dispersed, geography can be used in another and unusual way: as an additional organizational dimension (see Figure 8.4). Regional representatives (R_1, R_2, . . . , R_p) should have no managerial responsibility

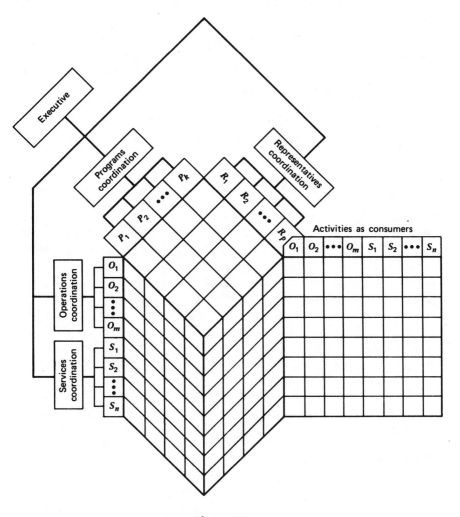

Figure 8.4.

for programs or activities. They should serve as representatives (advocates) of those who are affected by the outputs and activities of the organization as a whole. They serve external stakeholders. They can evaluate programs and activities in each region from the point of view of those outside the organization who are affected by them. These evaluations can be fed back to the organization's executive, coordinators, and unit directors.

By calling together the regional representatives, any program director can obtain an overall picture of his program's performance across the area it serves and in each region. This enables him to allocate his resources across regions more effectively.

Geography is not the only criterion that can be used to classify external stakeholders. Many other criteria can be used. For example, a company that supplies a variety of different industries—say, with lubricants—may find it useful to have advocates for industries rather than regions. They might be designated as automotive, aerospace, machine-tool, and so on. A public service organization may define its advocates' responsibility by the socioeconomic characteristics of the recipients of the services.

SOME VARIATIONS

The MD organizational design presented here is, as previously noted, a theme around which many variations can be written, variations that are responsive to the unique characteristics of an organization's mission or environment. Only two such variations are described here.

A recently prepared design of the national health and welfare services in Iran involves a three-dimensional organizational structure (programs, operations, and services) for each of the regions into which the country is divided. The smaller regions are not provided with all the operations and services they require, but they can buy these from larger neighboring regions. The regional executives report directly to the minister. This design, originally stimulated by a desire to decentralize management and be more responsive to varying local needs, also provides the flexibility required in a rapidly changing society.

Another variant is to be found in the organization of the Industrial Management Institute of Tehran which designed the health and welfare system described above. The institute is divided into two parts, each a two-dimensional matrix of programs and operations. They share common services (see Figure 8.5). Operations can also be used as a common third dimension to any number—not necessarily two—of two-dimensional matrices.

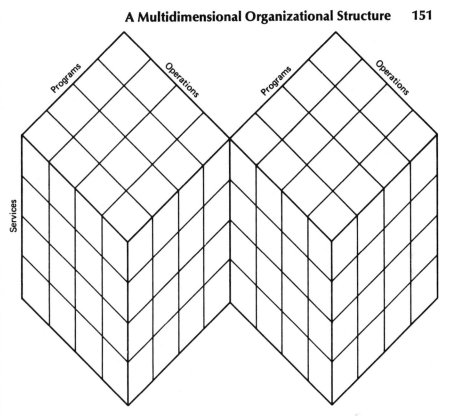

Figure 8.5.

SOME EXAMPLES

MD organizational design is not restricted to privately owned enterprises, as the examples in the last section show. Two additional examples follow.

A Government Agency

This example is based on a study done of and for CONASUPO, the National Basic Commodity Agency of the Mexican government. This agency operates with a budget slightly under $3 billion per year, employs about 14,000 persons, and is responsible for the production, distribution, processing, and sale of subsistence goods, particularly food.

The five programs incorporated into the design were defined by the organization's five objectives:

1. Increase the income of low-income producers of subsistence goods.

2. Increase the production of subsistence goods and the productivity of such production efforts.

3. Improve the quality of subsistence goods.

4. Increase the availability of (a) subsistence goods to low-income consumers and (b) supplies and services required to produce them.

5. Increase the purchasing power of (a) low-income consumers for subsistence goods and (b) low-income producers of such goods for the supplies and services required to produce them.

Seven operations were identified:

1. Buying (raw materials)
2. Transporting
3. Producing
4. Storing
5. Selling, leasing, and lending
6. Financing and insuring
7. Educating and developing intended beneficiaries

Nine services were identified:

1. Information services
2. Legal services
3. Accounting and control
4. Research and development
5. Personnel services
6. Purchasing (supplies and services), personnel, transportation, and maintenance
7. Public relations
8. Construction and production of facilities and equipment
9. General services

Programs were further broken down using *subsistence classes*, that is, food, clothing, health products, and shelter and furnishings. Operations were also broken down using subsistence classes and geography. In addition, use was made of ten regional representatives whose advocacy function is described above.

A coordinator was used for programs, another for operations, and a third for services. There was also a coordinator of regional representatives. The coordinators reported directly to the executive.

This design was modified slightly by CONASUPO executives to minimize the number of changes required in the current organization without sacrificing the essential features of the design. Although the resulting design of the organization as a whole has yet to be implemented, a three-dimensional design of ICONSA, the production subsidiary of CONASUPO, has been completed and is in the process of implementation.

Universities

The output units of a university can be defined by the types of degree awarded. Each of these, of course, is already called a "program." Research institutes or centers defined by subject matter, extracurricular programs, and athletic programs may also be included. Operating units consist primarily of academic departments coordinated by colleges. Service units include the library, computing center, printing services, financial and accounting departments, buildings and grounds, and so on.

In a university so organized, academic programs receive income from tuition or by vouchers turned in by students and cashed by the university's subsidizer, if it is subsidized. Program benefit measures are some function of the number of degrees awarded. Therefore, they can be profit-and-loss centers. Research programs require other types of measure, but they too can be profit-and-loss centers.

Academic programs buy teaching time and research programs buy research time from departments whose only income comes from the sale of their services. If a program director is dissatisfied with a department's services, he can buy the services from another university or finance another department's development of the ability to provide the service he wants. Departments, on the other hand, can sell their services outside the university, for example, to corporate educational programs or other universities.

This arrangement prevents the control of a program by any one or a combination of departments, and it encourages interdisciplinary activities.

The presence of tenured faculty in departments whose time cannot be sold to programs creates a special problem. Unless tenure is modified, it may be necessary for a department to be subsidized to cover its unsalable and nondisposable faculty members. However, at least this would be explicit, and the executive would know where the academic deadwood is and how much it costs.

The charges made by a department for its services would be over-headed to cover its administrative costs and to provide it with some development funds.

Service units would also sell their services to programs, departments, and to the executive function.

The National Autonomous University of Mexico (UNAM) recently opened three new colleges on separate and dispersed campuses each of which has a design similar to the one described here. The financing of units, however, is a compromise between the conventional budgeting of departments and the type of program budgeting described here. However, the University plans to move toward this type of program budgeting. In the new colleges now being constructed and planned, the University intends to take further steps in this direction.

ON DIVIDED RESPONSIBILITY

The MD organization presented here has something in common with what has been called "matrix organizations" (see Davis and Lawrence, 1977), but matrix organizations are normally two dimensional and lack many of the essential features of the design discussed, particularly the financial features. However, they do *appear* to have one deficiency in common: those people in activity units appear to work for two bosses, and this is generally taken to be undesirable. It is the most frequently cited deficiency of matrix organizations and is said to be the cause of what might be called "occupational schizophrenia."

The MD design creates no such problem, although the matrix organization may. In an MD organization members of an activity unit whose activities have been purchased by a program director are related to that director no differently than if he were an external customer. They are responsible to the activity unit director who, naturally, will use the program director's evaluation of his subordinates' performance in his evaluation of them. One who heads an activity unit's service group working for a program is in much the same position as a project director in a construction or a consulting firm. There is no ambiguity about who his boss is, but he does have to deal with a program director as a customer. There is nothing new or difficult about such a situation. As a director of research projects carried out by a university-based group for external sponsors, I am in exactly this position. The dean of my college is my boss, not any of my sponsors. The sponsors, however, have considerable control over what I do, and the dean is well aware of how they evaluate my services.

MD DESIGN AND PROGRAM BUDGETING

The intersection and divergence of some of the ideas incorporated into the MD organizational design and the ideas contained in "program budgeting" deserve some comment. Program budgeting, as normally promoted and practiced, is only a way of preparing a budget for activities and programs; it is *not* associated with giving resources and choices to program units or with requiring activities to earn their way in an internal and external market place. In brief, program budgeting normally does not contain an *organizational* idea and has no effect on organizational flexibility; it is a way of allocating resources to activities that provide greater assurance that programs will be carried out. In addition, it provides a more effective way than is usually available for determining the costs of programs. An MD design accomplishes all that a program budget does and much more.

CONCLUSION

The organizational design presented here is intended to increase organizational flexibility and responsiveness to changing internal and external conditions. It does this by dividing the organization into units whose survival depends on their ability to produce at a competitive price goods and services that are in demand. It creates a market place *within* an organization whether it be public or private, for profit or not. This increases responsiveness to both internal and external customers. Because units in an MD organization are relatively independent of one another, they can be added, subtracted, or otherwise modified more easily than in most conventional organizations. The performance measure of each unit is decoupled from that of any other. This makes it easier for the executive to evaluate and control the units. Even the executive function can be evaluated separately. It is accountable for all its actions.

The design is also resistant to the development of bureaucracy. It is not possible for operating units or programs to be victimized by service units whose procedures become ends in themselves and obstructions to the pursuit of organizational objectives. Users, inside and outside the organization, control internal suppliers. Suppliers are never in control of users. The organization is ends not means oriented. Bureaucracy is characterized by the subordination of ends to means.

The MD design is not a panacea or a cure-all. Man cannot conceive of an organization that some are not capable of subverting. Although the MD design removes some of stimuli to subversion found in many conventional organizations, it does not remove all of them. By itself the design gives no assurance of enriched and rewarding work at the lower levels of the organization, but the design makes it easier to apply other new ideas that are relevant to organizational development, such as worker participation and self-determination, a scheme for which is presented in the next chapter.

The MD design is not the only way of increasing organizational flexibility and responsiveness to change, but thinking seriously about it increases flexibility and responsiveness of thinking about organizations. This, hopefully, will lead to new and superior organizational designs.

CHAPTER NINE

Participation Within Organizations

In Chapter 5 we noted that the doctrine of participative management or organizational democracy seems to give rise to a dilemma. Complex task-oriented groups require a hierarchical organization if they are to accomplish their tasks efficiently. A division of labor is required, and the coordination of divided labor is essential. This necessitates organizational levels and hierarchy. Hierarchy implies that authority flows down and responsibility up. Each member of the organization is responsible to those above him and has authority over those who are responsible to him. Therefore, the concepts *superior* and *subordinate* play a central role in organizations. Democracy, on the other hand, implies that the ultimate authority is the "committee of the whole"—the public in the case of government—and everyone in authority is subject to control by those over whom he has authority.

Now how can democracy and participation fit into a hierarchy without destroying it? The horns of this dilemma can be escaped by the use of *circular organizations,* ones in which the conventional constraint requiring one-directional flow of authority, "down," is violated.

In organizations of any size, the large number of decisions required makes it infeasible to involve every member of the organization in every decision. Some division of decision-making labor is essential if for no other reason than that no one can know enough to make all the decisions required as effectively as is required for the survival of the

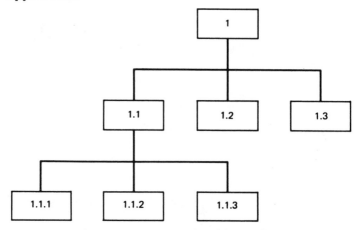

Figure 9.1. A conventional hierarchy.

organization. It is possible, however, to involve each member of an organization in the decisions of their immediate superiors and to provide them with some control over these superiors. This can be done by the use of "Boards" to which each manager reports.

Consider a small, traditionally designed organization such as that shown in Figure 9.1. In many such organizations, public or private, the highest executive, 1, reports to a board. This board generally has two principal functions: first, it *evaluates the performance* of the chief executive who reports to it, and, second, it sets *policies* within which he manages. The board does *not* manage; it monitors and controls the chief executive.

This concept can be generalized by providing each manager with a board that performs similar functions. First, however, let us consider the composition of these boards and then its functions.

The key to circularly designed organizations lies in the composition of the boards (see Figure 9.2). Consider the intermediate level manager, 1.1, as an example. Each manager, in this case 1.1, is a member of the board to which he reports. This ensures effective communication between him and his board. His immediate superior, in this case 1, is also a member of his board. This avoids divided authority over any manager. (The chief executive, 1, is a special case which we consider in a moment.) In addition, each manager who reports directly to the manager whose board we are constructing is also a member of his board. In this case managers 1.1.1, 1.1.2, and 1.1.3 are members of 1.1's board. (The lowest-level manager's board is also a special case which is considered later.)

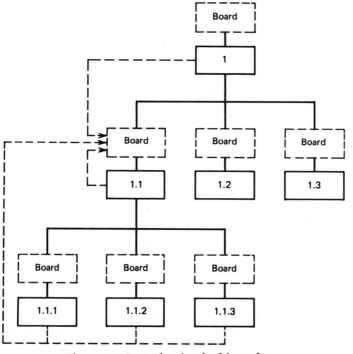

Figure 9.2. Part of a circular hierarchy.

Note that each manager except the chief executive is a member of his superior's board.

Before considering the top and bottom levels, which are special cases, let us focus on manager 1.1. He is a member of the board to which he reports and a member of the board to which his immediate superior, 1, reports. He is also a member of the boards to which each of his immediate subordinates report.

Each board may be chaired by the senior member, or a rotating chairmanship may be used.

A manager who has two or more levels of management above and below him will interact with *five* levels of management, his own and the two above and the two below him. This provides him with an extended vertical view of the organization, both up and down. This ensures the vertical integration of management within the organization.

In the board of his superior, each manager interacts with all other managers at his level who report to the same superior. This ensures horizontal coordination. The coordination of his subordinates takes place in his board, and of their subordinates in their boards.

The boards thus make possible a degree of vertical integration and horizontal coordination of management that is not normally possible in conventional hierarchies.

Now consider the lowest-level manager, for example, 1.1.1. His board consists of himself, his superior, 1.1, and *all* those who work under him, even though they are not managers. This obviously requires that the size of the ultimate organizational units be small enough to have a workable "committee of the whole" in which those at the bottom of the hierarchy can participate meaningfully. It also ensures units small enough so that each member can be treated as an individual by his superior.

The board of the chief executive, 1, includes him and those who report directly to him—1.1, 1.2, and 1.3. It should also include representatives of those at the bottom of the hierarchy—this completes the circle—and of each other level of the organization. These representatives should be elected by those at each level. The representatives of the workers at the bottom should not be union representatives. The top board is not the appropriate place for labor-management negotiations. It may, however, set policies that affect labor-management relations.

The top board should also include representatives of the principal external "stakeholders," those who are affected by the activities of the organization but are not part of it. For example, in a private corporation these would include consumers, investors and creditors, suppliers, and the general public. No group of stakeholders, internal or external, should constitute a majority of the board and be able to control corporate policy.

One group within the organization has not yet been dealt with: the staffs of the managers. If the staff is small enough, all its members can serve on their superior's board but collectively have only one vote. If they are too large for such participation, they should elect a representative who serves on the relevant board.

The boards, as noted, are *not* managing committees; they do not replace the manager. They have two responsibilities. First, they evaluate the performances of the managers who report to them. They can remove the man who occupies a managerial job from that job, but they cannot fire him. Only his boss can do that. Thus, if they do remove a man from his managerial post, his boss must decided what to do with him. This means that no man can occupy a position of authority without the support of his subordinates who constitute a majority of his board. He can in turn fire any of his subordinates. This is the essence of circular control. It requires that those in authority be capable of leadership and be competent. Support from above is not sufficient to keep them in their jobs.

Second, the boards set policies that control the operations of the managers reporting to them. Policies are not decision; they are *decision rules*. For example, a policy may dictate that no one who is not a college graduate can be appointed to certain posts. The selection of an individual to fill such a post is a decision.

Policies made at any board below the top must be consistent with policies made by higher-level boards. Any board can request a revision of higher-level policy. Since the senior member of each board is a member of boards at two higher levels, he can serve as its spokesman at the relevant higher level.

The kind of boards described here would ensure responsiveness to the needs and desires of both those within the organization and those in its environment who are affected by it.

In practice such boards meet no more than twice per month. Meetings are usually one to three hours duration. Therefore, if the number of subordinates reporting to a manager is restricted to no more than nine, the number generally accepted as the maximum that yields an effective span of control, a manager would be a member of no more than eleven boards. If the meetings of a board average four hours per month, a maximum of forty-four hours per month would be spent in board meetings, about twenty-five percent of a manager's time.

When a chief executive of a company that has a circular organization was asked when he gets his work done since he has to spend so much time in board meetings, he replied: "In the board meetings. You should have asked what I do with the rest of my time."

The organizational design presented here is only meant to serve as a theme around which many variations can and should be written to match the unique conditions that pertain in each organization. The concept of circularity must itself be treated creatively.

CHAPTER TEN

The Effect of Advertising on Sales:
A Study of Relations*

In this case study, the relationship between the amount spent on advertising, its timing, media usage, and sales of a consumer product, beer, is explored experimentally in some depth. The case reveals how research can be used to illuminate such relationships and how complex and counterintuitive they may be. The simple relational assumptions that go into many advertising decisions can be very costly and reduce their effectiveness significantly.

Just before mid-1961, Mr. August A. Busch, Jr., then President and Chairman of the Board of Anheuser-Busch, Inc., asked my colleagues and I if we could evaluate an advertising decision he was about to make. In that year Budweiser, the largest selling beer in the United States, was budgeted to receive about $15 million worth of advertising. Mr. Busch had been approached by the vice president of marketing with a request for an additional $1,200,000 to be spent on advertising in twelve marketing areas. The vice president had defended his proposal on the basis of a projected increase in sales that he believed it would produce. Mr. Busch explained that he was confronted with such a proposal every year and that he always accepted it. He intended to do the same again, but, he asked, "Is there some way I can find out at the end of the year whether I got what I paid for?" We said we would think about it and come back with some suggestions.

The proposal we presented to Mr. Busch shortly thereafter consisted

* This case is adapted from Ackoff and Emshoff (Winter, 1975).

of allowing the marketing department to select any six of the twelve areas it wanted and giving it $600,000 for additional advertising. The remaining six areas would not be touched and would be used as "controls." This biased selection procedure was intended to overcome some of the opposition that the marketing department had to any effort to evaluate its proposal.

Earlier we had developed an equation for forecasting monthly sales in each marketing area. Our plan was to measure the deviation of actual monthly sales from the forecast for each marketing area in the test. Using the statistical characteristics of the forecasts, we estimated that we had a ninety-five percent chance of detecting a four percent increase in sales in the areas with additional advertising. Since the increase predicted by the marketing department was in excess of this amount, Mr. Busch authorized the test, and it was initiated.

The test was conducted over the last six months of 1961 yielding seventy-two (12 × 6) observations. *The analysis of these data failed to reveal any significant difference between the test and control areas.* Nevertheless the control areas did better on average than was forecast. Therefore, we assumed that all the sales above those forecast were attributable to the increased advertising and evaluated the results accordingly. Even under this assumption the increased amount of advertising was *not* justified by the deliberately overestimated increase in sales attributed to it.

Encouraged by these results, Mr. Busch asked us to design research directed at determining what amount *should be* spent on advertising. He wanted to proceed with caution, however, because he believed that much of Budweiser's success—it was leading the beer market with a share of 8.14 percent in 1962—was due to its quality and the effectiveness with which this was communicated through its advertising. When we suggested research involving experimentation with marketing areas, he authorized use of fifteen such areas provided they did not include any of the company's major markets.

Constrained in this way, we sought an experimental design that would maximize learning about advertising expenditures. Our design effort was guided by two methodological principles. First, we knew that the company advertised for only one reason: *to increase sales.* Therefore, we were determined to measure the effect of advertising on sales and not, as is usually done, on one or more easily measured intervening variables such as recall of messages or attitudes toward the product. For this reason we decided to continue to use deviations of actual from forecast sales as the variable to be observed. This allowed us to cancel out much of the effect on sales of factors other than advertising. Therefore, efforts to improve forecasting of monthly market-ing-area sales were continuous.

Second, we were committed to an attempt to *explain* the causal effect of advertising on consumer purchases, not merely to find statisti-cal correlations between them. Our search of the marketing literature for such an explanation was futile; all it uncovered were correlations and regressions (associations) between advertising and sales. These usually showed that increases (or decreases) in the former were asso-ciated with increases (or decreases) in the latter. From such associations it was almost universally inferred, *incorrectly*, that increases in advertis-ing *produce* increases in sales almost without limit. We believed that these analyses really showed that most companies forecast next year's sales quite accurately and that they set their advertising budgets as a fixed percentage of predicted sales. Put another way: forecasts of in-creased sales produce increased advertising.

Our commitment to experimentation derived from a determination to find a *causal* connection between advertising and sales, not merely an association between them: to develop an ability to manipulate ad-vertising to produce the desired effects on sales that could be observed.

Since we had no tested theory to go on, we fabricated our own. Our hunch was that advertising could be considered to be a *stimulus* and sales a *response* to it. A great deal is known about the general nature of stimulus-response functions. They usually take the form shown in Figure 10.1. Therefore, we formulated the following hypothesis:

> A small amount of advertising has virtually no effect on sales, but as the amount is increased it pushes the response through a *threshold* after which it produces an increasing effect. This effect decreases and flattens out once the respondents are *saturated;* that is, they either turn off further exposure to the stimulus or are consuming up to their capabilities or capacities. A response to further increases in advertising remains relatively unchanged until the respondents reach *supersaturation,* a "fed-up" point beyond which they respond negatively.

In an earlier study we had done for the Lamp Division of the Gen-eral Electric Company (Waid, Clark, and Ackoff, 1956) we found such a relationship between the frequency of sales calls (stimuli) and pur-chases (responses). In the sales-call context, the idea of *supersaturation* is not as shocking as it is in advertising. Clearly there is an amount of a salesman's presence that is intolerable to a buyer. Beyond this, one would expect the buyer to try to get rid of the salesman by discontinu-ing his purchases. Similarly, we felt reasonably sure that if, for example,

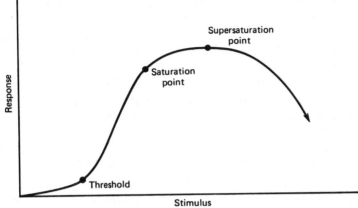

Figure 10.1. A typical stimulus-response function.

all television advertising were for one product, the public would react negatively.

A minimal experiment would have involved applying the same percentage change in advertising expenditures to each of the fifteen marketing areas allotted to us and comparing the results obtained from them with those obtained from an equal number of control (unchanged) areas. However, we needed only nine areas to obtain the level of accuracy set as our target: to be able to detect a two percent difference in sales ninety-five percent of the time. To introduce two different treatments—one involving an increase and the other a decrease in advertising expenditures—required eighteen test areas, three more than were available. However, even an experiment with two different treatments would yield only three points: the average effect of each treatment and that of the control group. The difficulty this presented derived from the fact that every configuration of three points except one, V-shaped, could be fitted to the relationship we wanted to test. Therefore, there was a very low probability that a three-level experiment would *dis*confirm our hypothetical relationship; thus it was a very poor test of the validity of this relationship.

For these reasons we decided to ask for three different treatments and a control group, even though this would require twenty-seven marketing areas plus nine under control. Four experimental points could disconfirm our theory as easily as it could confirm it and hence would have provided a reasonable test of it.

We had nothing to go on but our intuition in selecting the experimental treatment levels: a fifty percent reduction and a fifty and 100 percent increase in budgeted levels of advertising. We wanted to make changes large enough to produce observable effects on sales, assuming such changes had any effect; thus, if there were no observable effects, this fact could not be dismissed because the changes were believed to be too small. Two increases rather than decreases were selected to make the experiment more palatable to the marketing department.

When this four-level design was presented, it was rejected because it involved the use of too many marketing areas. Mr. Busch agreed, however, to our use of eighteen (rather than fifteen) areas *provided* that we changed the reduction in advertising from fifty to twenty-five percent. He felt that a fifty percent reduction might irreparably damage the areas so treated. This left us with a three-level experiment: minus twenty-five, zero, and fifty percent changes from budget.

We were not completely happy with this outcome, because it did not provide an adequate test of our theory, but we were pleased that we had the opportunity to conduct even a limited experiment. We were reasonably sure that if it produced "interesting" results, restrictions on future experiments would be lifted.

A 3 × 3 × 3 factorially designed experiment was prepared in which two other important marketing variables were explicitly controlled: *the amount spent on sales effort* (on salesmen) and *the amount spent on point-of-sales materials* (displays, signs, etc.) (see Figure 10.2). We would also have liked to control *pricing*, but this was precluded.

Marketing areas were selected randomly from the "permissable list" and randomly assigned to the twenty-seven treatments. The use of this list could obviously bias our results, but again our hope was that the results would justify further experiments and that they would not be so restricted.

The experiment was carried out over twelve months, yielding twelve observations of each marketing area. We were able to reach a conclusion at the end of six months, but the experiment was continued to build up confidence in the results. This did not work, however, because the results were too much at variance with expectations within the company and its advertising agency. The three points shown in Figure 10.3 fell into the only configuration, V-shaped, that was inconsistent with our hypothesis because the relationship being tested had no V in it. In addition, we found no significant interaction between advertising, sales effort, and point-of-sales expenditures—a surprising but not unacceptable result—and that current levels of sales effort and point-of-sales expenditures were close to optimal. The last result was readily accepted.

No one found much difficulty in believing that a fifty percent in-

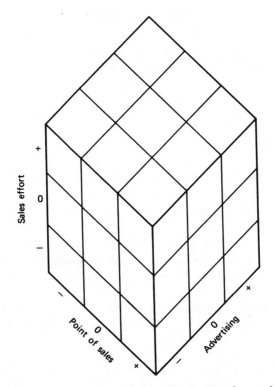

Figure 10.2. A 3 × 3 × 3 factorially designed experiment.

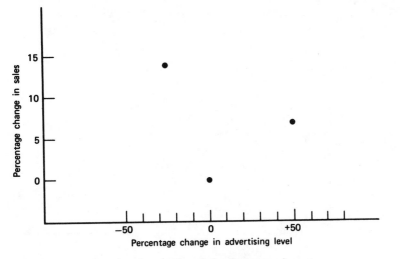

Figure 10.3. Results of the first experiment.

crease in advertising produced a seven percent increase in sales, but only Mr. Busch and Mr. Vogel, the new vice president of marketing, were willing to consider seriously the possibility that a twenty-five percent reduction of advertising could produce a fourteen percent increase in sales. Even they were not ready to act on this finding, but they wanted to take a "closer look." They asked us to design another experiment that would check these results and would be more convincing to others.

We had to set our theory straight before designing the next experiment. The preceding experiment appeared to reject the theory, but we had grown fond of it, perhaps because so many who were supposed to be in "the know" thought it was ridiculous. Thus we sought a modification of the theory that would make it consistent with the experimental results.

It occurred to us that there might be two or more distinct consuming populations in each marketing area and that each had a response curve like the one we had assumed but that these were separated along a horizontal scale (as shown in Figure 10.4). Then the aggregated response curve would have a V in it. When this possibility was presented to Mr. Vogel, he thought it quite reasonable and suggested that the markets might be segmented into three parts: heavy, moderate, and light beer drinkers. This made sense to us. One would expect the heavy users of a product to be more sensitive to its advertising than moderate users, and the moderate users, to be more sensitive than light users. We looked for some way of testing this assumption and found one.

It would have been very time consuming and costly to determine how many beer drinkers of each type there were in each marketing

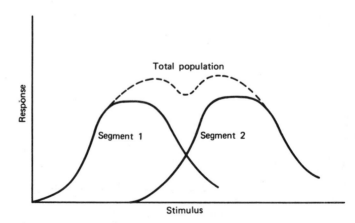

Figure 10.4. Response function of segmented population.

area. We had neither the time nor the money required to do so. However, we did know from previous studies that beer consumption correlated positively with discretionary income within the range of income in which most beer drinkers fall. Thus we determined the average discretionary income in each marketing area that had been used in the previous experiment and compared it with the average deviations from forecast sales in each area. There was a positive correlation between these deviations and average discretionary income, lending some credence to the user-level segmentation assumption.

We revised our theory to incorporate three response functions for each marketing area. This meant that the aggregated response functions for markets as a whole could differ significantly because of different proportions of heavy, moderate, and light beer drinkers.

Armed with this revised theory, we decided that we would like seven different advertising treatments so that we could adequately test it. We wanted to replicate the earlier experiment and add treatments further out on both sides of the scale. Seven treatments were selected: minus one hundred percent (no advertising), minus fifty, minus twenty-five, zero, fifty, one hundred, and two hundred percent. Because of improvements in our forecasting methods, only six areas were required for each treatment. This design was accepted with only slight modification: the number of test areas in the two extreme treatments was reduced.

This experiment was also conducted over a twelve-month period. Fortunately, the results obtained from the treatments that had been used in the first experiment were the same as in the earlier experiment. When plotted, the seven points fell on a curve such as the one shown in Figure 10.5. There were two deviations from our expectations. First, only two, not three, "humps" appeared. We did not take this seriously, because the points out on the right were so far apart that there could well be a third hump concealed by the interpolation between the points. It was harder to explain the finding that the areas in which all advertising had been eliminated survived the year with no significant difference in performance from the control areas. Hardly anyone believed this result. The believers attributed it to the long history, strength, and exposure of Budweiser in the market place. We suggested further tests of the effect of complete elimination of advertising.

There was no such problem with the areas that had received a two hundred percent increase in advertising. The distributors in these areas complained constantly during the experiment about the overexposure and the unfavorable feedback they were getting from the "trade" and consumers.

Mr. Vogel and we agreed that the generally negative, if not hostile,

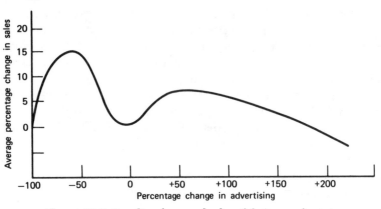

Figure 10.5. Results of second advertising experiment.

reception of the research by the company's advertising agencies derived from the fact that their income was threatened by the results.
They were paid in the conventional way: a fixed percentage of the
amount spent by the company on advertising. This struck us as irrational, because it discouraged the agency from acting in the company's
best interests. A change was made in the way of compensating the
agencies. A scheme was developed by which agency fees were increased if sales increased with no increase in advertising or advertising
decreased with no decrease in sales. This provided an incentive that
encouraged the agency to collaborate in the research effort and to
initiate its own research. The income of the Budweiser agency bene-
fitted from this change. It has since initiated such a compensation
scheme with some of its other clients.

Although a willingness to act on our findings had not yet developed,
there was growing agreement on the desirability of continuing the research. The second experiment was continued with particular attention
to the areas from which all advertising had been removed. The objective was to determine how long it would take before any deterioration
of sales could be detected and at what rate it would take place. We
also wanted to determine how much effort would be required to recap-
ture lost sales.

At the same time research was initiated into the relative effectiveness
of different media. While this research was going on, the first opportunity to apply results from the earlier work presented itself.

Mr. Busch wanted to make more cash available to meet some commitments he had made. He asked Mr. Vogel and us if this could be done.
We jointly proposed that advertising be reduced by fifteen percent in

twenty-five of the smallest markets. The markets were chosen to mini-mize any possible long-run harmful effects. The proposed changes were capable of yielding more than the amount Mr. Busch needed. We also pointed out that we could maintain very close watch over the areas affected and report immediately on any reduction of sales that might occur in them. We predicted, however, that the proposed de-crease in advertising would produce about a five percent increase in sales. Despite his sketicism about the increase, Mr. Busch decided to go ahead.

The predicted results were obtained within six months. As a conse-quence, the number of "reduction areas" was increased to fifty and the amount of the reductions was increased to twenty-five percent. From then on, more and more areas were similarly treated, and the reduc-tions were gradually increased until the advertising expenditure per barrel was $0.80 in contrast to $1.89 when the research was initiated. During this period (1962–1968), sales of Budweiser increased from ap-proximately 7.5 million to 14.5 million barrels, and its market share in-creased from 8.14 to 12.94 percent.

Returning to the experiment that involved complete deprivation of advertising, the areas thus deprived showed no response until *more than a year and a half* after the experiment was initiated. From then on a small decline was noted each month. This was allowed to continue only long enough to provide good estimates of the deterioration rate. Moves to correct these markets were then made. The markets were re-stored to their normal growth rate in about six months with only their normal amount of advertising.

These results led to a new line of speculation. Would it not be pos-sible to *pulse* advertising, using an off-and-on pattern, and obtain the same effectiveness as that obtained by continuous advertising? We came to think of advertising as a motion picture which, of course, is really a sequence of motionless pictures. If sixteen still photographs are taken and projected per second, the appearance of motion is created because images are retained in the retina between exposures. We felt the same should be true for advertising.

Two types of pulsing were considered. In one, advertising expendi-tures in all media are off or on together. In the other, only one medium is used at any time, but the media are alternated. We designed an ex-periment to test the first of these types of pulse. It involved four treat-ments: one control (I) and three pulsing patterns (II, III, and IV), as shown in Table 10.1. In addition, the level of expenditure in each was varied, as shown in Table 10.2. The marketing areas used in this experi-ment were classified by median income and growth rates.

Table 10.1. Pulsing Patterns

	I	II	III	IV
Spring	x	x	o	x
Summer	x	o	x	x
Fall	x	x	o	o
Winter	x	o	x	o

Table 10.2. Percentage of Local Budget Spent by Pulsing Pattern and Advertising Level

Advertising Level	Pulsing Pattern (%)			
	I	II	III	IV
High	150	100	100	100
Low	100	50	50	50

One of the pulsing patterns was found to be significantly better than the others and slightly better than normal advertising when accompanied by a high level of expenditure. Another pattern was found to be best when accompanied by a low level of expenditure.

The pulsing patterns were found to interact significantly with median income level and the growth rate of the market area. Subsequent experimentation revealed no significant difference between time pulsing and media pulsing, but media pulsing was easier to administer.

These results were cautiously incorporated into small reductions of advertising expenditures that were made in series. It was only after one change was demonstrated to have the predicted effect that the next change was made. Regular monthly checks on the performance of each marketing area were initiated and continue to this day.

In the early experiments on advertising expenditures, the budgets for experimental areas were set by the research team, but the way additional moneys were allocated to media or reductions made was left entirely to the advertising agency. Five media were involved: billboards, magazines, newspapers, radio, and television. We analyzed the relationship between the actual changes in media allocations made by the agency and changes in sales in each marketing area. This preliminary analysis indicated no significant differences between magazines, newspapers, and radio, but it suggested that television was slightly superior and that billboards were substantially inferior.

Table 10.3. Media Experiment: Number and Treatments of Marketing Areas

	Local TV	Billboard	Radio	Newsaper
No national TV	5	5	5	5
National TV	5	5	5	5

An experiment was designed to test these tentative findings (see Table 10.3). Magazines were not included in this experiment because they could not be controlled within small areas. (They were investigated separately at a later date.) A distinction was made between local and national television. In each of twenty areas only one medium was used; in another twenty each medium was combined with national television.

The results showed that national television was slightly superior to any local medium. Local television (with or without national television) and radio were more effective than newspapers or billboards. Billboards were the least effective. This required explanation.

First, a number of observations were made to determine how much information could be conveyed by a billboard. We found that little more than the product name and a slogan could be conveyed. This meant that billboards could do little more than remind one of the existence of an already familiar product; they cannot convey much new information. Our second set of observations showed that the typical urban dweller in the United States saw (but did not necessarily notice) the word Budweiser on signs, displays, or beer containers almost ten times per day. He hardly needed additional reminding of its existence. On the basis of these findings virtually all billboard advertising was discontinued. The company had been spending about twenty percent of its advertising budget on this medium.

It would be foolish, of course, to claim that the improvement in company performance was due entirely to changes in advertising. Other types of changes, some based on research and some not, were also made during this period. One thing is clear: the changes induced by the research described here did not hurt Anheuser-Busch.

A little bit of understanding can go a long way, but one may have to go a long way to get a little bit of understanding.

CHAPTER ELEVEN

Why People Drink:
Toward Understanding Objectives*

Understanding human behavior, particularly consuming behavior, is obviously of value to those who provide the products consumed. Few of us understand why we behave as we do, but we are convinced that we have such understanding. Our explanations of our own behavior are often excuses and rationalizations of it. This would be bad enough but, in addition, we tend to infer from our self-misunderstanding to misunderstanding of others. Correct explanations of human behavior, even partial explanations, are often very difficult to come by, even when the behavior involved is commonplace.

In the study described here an explanation was sought for the consumption of alcoholic beverages, a very commonplace event the explanation of which is far from commonplace. This study followed on the heels of the one reported in the last chapter and was also done for Anheuser-Busch, Inc.

Early in 1968 Mr. E. H. Vogel, Jr., then Vice President of Marketing, with whom the work reported in Chapter 11 had been done, asked that we turn our attention to the content of advertising: the quality of messages. We began by surveying organizations that offered message-evaluation services. A great deal of information was collected about each. Using this we selected for closer examination about a half dozen of these organizations, those which most impressed us on paper. We then visited each one and went over their procedures in detail. Finally,

*Russel L. Ackoff and James R. Emshoff, "Advertising Research at Anheuser-Busch, Inc. (1968–74)." Sloan Management Review, Spring 1975, pp. 1–15. Reprinted by permission.

we selected the agency that seemed to us to have the soundest procedures, and we made this proposition to it: we would carry out an experimental evaluation of its message evaluations with the understanding that, if the results were favorable, it could use them as it saw fit; if
they were not, we would not release information about the study that
would identify the organization. The agency agreed.

A-B's principal advertising agency was asked to select fifty of its
television comercials equally divided into those it considered to be
among its best and its worst. The advertising agency was not restricted
to selecting commercials that had actually been used.

The message-evaluation agency was then asked to conduct tests of
these commercials in three cities selected by us. It was to identify six
commercials that were evaluated as superior and six that were evaluated as inferior in all three cities.

The agency obtained consistent evaluations in two of the three
cities, but the third yielded results that were inconsistent with the other
two. The city causing the trouble was one in which A-B had a large
brewery. We began to suspect that the message evaluations obtained
in this city were greatly influenced by the company's presence.
Through discussion with others who had conducted similar message
evaluations, we learned that they had had similar experiences in cities
in which a company was a major economic force. This suggested that
most of the public in such cities already had strong opinions, one way
or the other, of the company and its products; hence they were not
subject to significant influence by advertising.

This led to two actions. First, another city was selected to replace
the "brewery city" in the message-evaluation effort. Second, a sequence of carefully monitored reductions in advertising was introduced
in the brewery city. Reductions of about $250,000 in annual expendi-
tures were made over a relatively short time, with no effect on sales.

The message-evaluation agency, using the new "third" city, was able
to identify the required number of consistently "superior" and "inferior" commercials. These were then used in a designed experiment
in which a number of marketing areas were exposed to nothing but
the superior commercials, and an equal number were exposed to nothing but the inferior commercials. The amounts spent on advertising in
these areas were carefully controlled. The deviation of actual from
forecast sales was used as the measure of performance.

We found no significant differences between the performances of
the two sets of markets. We concluded that the message evaluations
were not related to the effectiveness of the messages, to their ability to
affect sales. The only positive value of this conclusion was that it led

A-B to discontinue its use of such message-evaluation services. This yielded a modest saving, but the problem originally put to us remained unsolved.

Before continuing with this account, it is worth pausing for a few observations. First, it should be noted how frequently we accept without question the ability of those who render a service to deliver what they promise. We tend to take such an ability for granted. If we require any evidence to support such a belief, we usually take the survival, success, or reputation of the server as sufficient. Such casual acceptance of expensive services can be a costly habit. The more obvious the value of a service appears to be, the more intensively it should be tested, if for no other reason than that its cost tends to be proportional to its "obviousness."

Second, note that an unexpected result (e.g., the behavior of the brewery city) usually presents an opportunity for improvement of performance if we can find an explanation of it. Many significant advances in science, for example, have been the result of looking into anomalies, misfitting observations. Now let us continue with the story.

Our experience with the message-evaluation agency convinced us that we would not be able to evaluate advertising messages adequately without knowing *why* people drink beer and, more generally, alcoholic beverages. When we mentioned this to a marketing manager in another company, he said it was perfectly clear why people drink beer: they like it. When we asked him how he knew this, he replied, "They wouldn't drink it if they didn't." We wanted a less circular and more illuminating "explanation" of drinking behavior.

We initiated an extensive literature search for theories purporting to explain alcohol consumption. All those we found dealt with the abuse rather than normal use of such beverages. Furthermore, not one of the theories had been adequately tested; most were based on a small number of clinical observations. To design and conduct adequate tests of these theories would have required more time, money, and patience than we had. Fortunately we found that someone else had already conducted such tests.

Dr. Fred E. Emery and his colleagues at the Human Resources Centre of The Tavistock Institute in London, with whom we had collaborated over a number of years, had tested most of the available theories with negative results. Emery and his co-workers then devoted their efforts to producing a detailed description of drinking behavior and to extracting from it underlying patterns that might provide a basis for theoretical speculation. They studied about 3000 regular drinkers in England, Ireland, and Norway. Their analysis disclosed three drinking types which Emery named and described somewhat as follows.

Reparative. These are generally middle aged and of either sex. They have not achieved as much as they had hoped to by that stage of their lives, although they are usually far from being failures. They believed they were capable of achieving what they wanted, but also believed that doing so would require sacrifice from others for whom they cared a great deal. For example, achievement might require a move that would displease wife and children. Therefore, they sacrificed their own aspirations in the interests of others but were well adjusted to this state.

Most reparative drinking occurs at the end of the work day rather than on weekends, vacations, or holidays. It usually takes place with a few close friends or members of the family. The reparative is a controlled drinker who seldom gets high or drunk and very rarely becomes an alcoholic. His or her drinking is associated with the transition from the work to the nonwork environment and is seen as a type of self-reward for sacrifices made for others.

Social. These are of either sex but are generally younger than reparative drinkers. They have not yet attained the levels of aspiration, but believe they will and that doing so requires approval and support of others. They are driven by ambition, the desire to get ahead.

Social drinking is heaviest on weekends, holidays, and vacations. It usually takes place in large groups consisting of acquaintances in social settings. The social is a controlled drinker but less so than the reparative. His or her drinking is associated with friendliness and acceptance of and by others. Alcoholic beverages are seen as lubricants of social situations.

Indulgent. These are of any age and either sex. They have not attained the levels of aspiration and never expect to. They consider themselves to be irretrievable failures. They view life as tragic.

The indulgent drinks most heavily when subjected to pressure to achieve. He or she drinks to escape such pressure. The indulgent is the least controlled drinker and is the most likely to get high or drunk and become an alcoholic.

We at Wharton found these categories to be exciting and suggestive, but we were disturbed by the fact that there were *three* of them. The only explanation for this could be that there was a single underlying scale on which the three categories represented low, medium, and high ranges. Emery and we agreed, however, that there must be more than one underlying scale. Even if there were only two, and each was minimally divided into two ranges (low and high), their combination would yield *four* types (low-low, low-high, high-low, and high-high).

We suspected that there were two underlying scales because two of Emery's drinking types appeared to be subtypes of two of four personality types that C. West Churchman and I had identified in the late 1940s. In our analysis of C. G. Jung's personality types, *introvert* and *extrovert*, Churchman and I had uncovered two underlying scales, hence four personality types of which introversion and extroversion were only two.

Introversion and extroversion deal with an individual's relationship with his environment. An individual is related to his environment in two ways: the way his environment affects him and the way he affects it. Churchman and I had constructed a scale on which measurements could be made of an individual's sensitivity to his environment. The probability of response was plotted against the strength of environmental stimuli (see Figure 11.1). The response space was divided in half by a diagonal from the lower left to the upper right. An individual all or most of whose probabilities of response fell above the diagonal was said to be sensitive to his or her environment because he or she was responsive to even weak environmental stimulation. He or she was called an *objectivert*. An individual all or most of whose probabilities

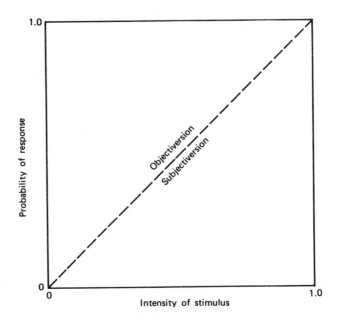

Figure 11.1. The environmental response function.

of response fell below the diagonal was insensitive to his environment. He was called a *subjectivert* because, if not responding to his environment, he had to be responding to something else, and what is not environment is *self*. Therefore, he is responsive to his own thoughts, feelings, beliefs, and attitudes.

An objectivert finds it easier to remember names, phone numbers, and addresses than a subjectivert. He or she will notice and remember furnishings or the dress of others and be more aware of their feelings and desires. The subjectivert thinks ahead, plans his or her activity, and tends to stick to the plan whatever happens; the objectivert tends not to plan but to respond to what happens. An objectivert is easily distracted by noise or other external stimuli and feels compelled to listen to anyone who speaks to him or her. A subjectivert tends to "turn off" distractions and frequently does not hear what is said to him or her and is often lost in his or her own thoughts.

Objectiversion and subjectiversion are tendencies, not rigid commitments. An objectivert may act like a subjectivert in some circumstances and vice versa. The less extreme a person's position in this space is, the more likely he is to respond to both internal and external stimuli. In some circumstances—for example, at a party—a subjectivert is likely to behave more like an objectivert than he usually does. On the other hand, an objectivert working alone in his or her office may look like a subjectivert.

A second scale was constructed that could be used to measure an individual's effect on his environment (see Figure 11.2). Here the cumulative probability of responding with varying degrees of effect on the environment is plotted. This space was also divided by a diagonal into two equal areas, one representing *internalization*—an inclination to act on oneself, to adapt oneself and modify one's own behavior to solve problems—and *externalization*—an inclination to act on and modify the environment in problem-solving efforts.

If someone enters an externalizer's environment and annoys or distracts him, he is likely to try to remove that person or get him to change his behavior. An internalizer in the same situation is more likely to try to ignore the intruder or move to another place. The externalizer tries to organize groups of which he is a part, to lead them; the internalizer is more likely to be a follower adapting to the wishes of the others. If a room gets cold the externalizer will try to turn up the heat or have someone else do it; the internalizer is more likely to add clothing.

Combining these two scales yields the four personality types shown in Figure 11.3. In our work in the 1940s, Churchman and I had observed that most people were neither introverts (subjective internalizers) nor

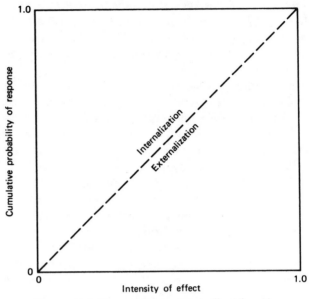

Figure 11.2. The environmental effect function.

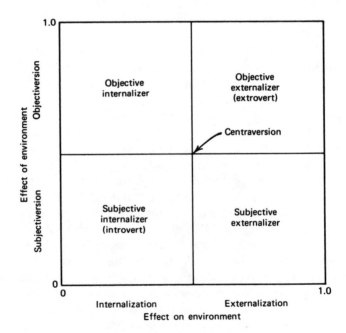

Figure 11.3. Personality types.

extroverts (objective externalizers) but one of the two *mixed* types (objective internalizers or subjective externalizers).

Now the initial hunch relating Emery's drinking types to our personality types was as follows.

1. Emery's *reparative* drinkers were *objective internalizers* because they were sensitive and responsive to the needs of others and adapted to them by sacrificing their unfulfilled aspirations. (Not all objective externalizers, of course, are drinkers, let alone reparative drinkers.)
2. Emery's *social* drinkers were *subjective externalizers* because they were primarily driven by their own ambitions and attempted to manipulate others to get what they wanted.

It also occurred to us that Emery's *indulgent* drinkers were divisible into two groups, corresponding to the two "pure" types, introvert and extrovert. If this were so, we hypothesized, introverted drinkers blamed their failures on the environment from which they were trying to escape by drinking; the extroverted drinkers blamed their failures on their own shortcomings and were trying to escape from consciousness of them. At our suggestion Emery reexamined his data on the indulgent and found that, indeed, the two drinking types we had inferred from our theory did exist. He retained the term *indulgent* for the introverted drinker and called the extroverted drinker an *oceanic*. This finding considerably reinforced our conviction that we were on the right track.

Emery had found that most regular drinkers were in the social and reparative groups, which were subclasses of our mixed types. Recall that Churchman and I had found that more people fell into the mixed types than into the pure types. This was also reinforcing.

In addition, Emery had found that most alcoholics were indulgents or oceanics (although most indulgents and oceanics were not alcoholics). Using our typology, we hypothesized two types of alcoholics. First, the introverted (indulgent) alcoholic who would tend to drink himself into a catatonic stupor with little or no consciousness of and interaction with his environment. He would tend to drink alone or with someone who would help protect his privacy. Second, the extroverted (oceanic) alcoholic who would tend to drink himself into un*self*-consciousness and hyperactivity, a manic or orgiastic state. We thought of the role played by Ray Milland in the motion picture, *The Lost Weekend,* as prototypical of the introverted alcoholic, and the type of orgiastic drinking shown in *La Dolce Vita* as prototypical of the extroverted alcoholic. Consistent with our theory was the fact that many orgies—for example, those associated with the Mardi Gras—involved

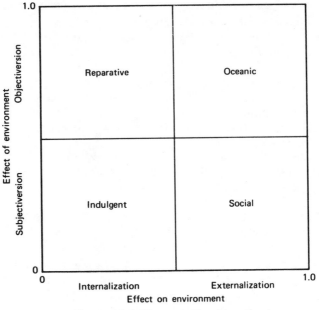

Figure 11.4. The matching hypothesis.

masks and costumes, which provide anonymity and facilitate escape from self. Subsequently, this hypothesis and others led us into studies of alcoholism that, however, are not an integral part of this story.

Our "matching hypothesis" (Figure 11.4)—that Emery's drinking types were subgroups of our personality types—required rigorous testing. This was done in a laboratory into which regular drinkers were brought for observation and interview. Since independent classifications of drinkers into the personality and drinking types were to be based in part on judgments made by clinical psychologists, it was first necessary to instruct them in the use of both classification schemes. Instruction and practice was continued until there was a high degree of consistency of judgments made independently by different clinicians, and these agreed with those made by the researchers responsible for the types and theory. Even after the interviewers were "calibrated," several independent judgments were made on each subject.

The results of one of the tests of the matching hypothesis, one that used 125 subjects, are shown in Table 11.1. Seventy-six percent of the observations fitted the hypothesis. This is relatively strong confirmation. Most of the mismatches, we believed, were due to lack of perfect precision in the classification procedures.

Table 11.1.   Results of a Test of the Matching Hypothesis (125 Subjects)

Drinking Types	Objective Internalizer (%)	Subjective Externalizer (%)	Objective Externalizer (%)	Subjective Internalizer (%)
Reparative	30	5	7	1
Social	4	31	1	3
Oceanic	0	1	10	0
Indulgent	1	0	1	5

Having established this link between the drinking types and the personality types, we began a more intensive research program to establish the causal links between our theory and the purposes served by the consumption of alcohol among the types. Before we could seek such an explanation, however, we had to develop and validate instruments for measuring the dimensions of our personality types. Although the clinical interviewing procedures had been demonstrated to have sufficient reliability, their cost was too great to employ them on larger samples drawn from multiple locations. Each of the 125 interviews cost approximately $300, and these were conducted in 1968. Even if we were to cut these costs in half, they would have been too large to enable us to deal with large samples in different locations. Consequently, we turned our research to the development of less expensive typing procedures. One direction we took involves the use of a behavioral laboratory in which we hoped to be able to reduce or eliminate clinical interviewing costs by collecting data on an individual's personality by observing his behavior in specially designed situations. The other direction we took involved the design of self-administered paper-and-pencil tests that a subject could take without supervision.

The behavioral situation we developed worked well; it provided rich and reliable readings on both personality scales, but the cost and the time required were too great, particularly when we had to operate in different cities. Nevertheless we found that the information obtained from this laboratory situation enabled us to design a substantially more efficient and shortened interviewing procedure to be used by the clinicians. Eventually we were able to obtain an accurate and reliable clinical typing of a subject for about $35.

The development of an acceptable self-administered paper-and-pencil test took more than two years. Two criteria of acceptability were imposed on this effort. First, there had to be at least a seventy-five percent agreement between the results of the test and clinical evaluations. Second, there was to be no bias in the classification of those subjects about whom there was disagreement between test and clinic. This would assure us of acceptable "collective" accuracy when we went into the field and used large numbers of subjects. Fortunately, A-B's management understood the methodological issues and did not press us into going into the field prematurely.

Once an acceptable test was developed, research could be directed to testing the hypotheses formulated to explain drinking behavior. The hypothesis formulated to do so was suggested by the earlier hypothesis about the two types of alcoholics and by the fact that most alcoholics came from the pure rather than the mixed types. In addition, it made use of the following intermediate "maturation hypothesis":

> As those in the pure types (introversion and extroversion) grow older they tend to become more introverted and extroverted, to move away from the point of centraversion. As those in the mixed types mature they tend to move toward centraversion.

By interviewing the spouses of middle- and older-aged couples in the clinic and extracting from each descriptions of the change in personality that had occurred in the other over the years, data were obtained that supported this hypothesis. This led to our "drinking hypothesis":

> Alcoholic beverages are used to produce short-run transformations in personality of the same type produced by maturation in the long run.

This hypothesis implies that introverts and extroverts drink to become more introverted and extroverted, respectively; however, the mixed types drink to become more centraverted.

We did not feel we could test this hypothesis by interviewing techniques, because we doubted that most drinkers were aware of their reasons for drinking (not to be confused with their rationalizations of it), and, if they were, they might be unwilling to reveal their reasons in an interview. Therefore, my colleague James Emshoff designed a rather complex but very effective behavioral test of this hypothesis.

Through a field survey, 250 regular drinkers were identified and invited to participate in an effort by Anheuser-Busch to select one of four newly developed beers to bring out on the market. They were invited to a meeting place at which, when they arrived, they were first given the paper-and-pencil personality-typing test previously referred to.

They were then told they would be given an opportunity to taste and test the four new beers, but before doing so they would be shown the television commercials that had been prepared for each brand.

The television commercials had been prepared by the advertising agency in story-board form. Each commercial consisted of three scenes. In the first a person who was clearly of one of the four personality types was shown in a situation that was characteristic of that type. In the second scene the same person was shown drinking one of the four new brands of beer while its virtues were extolled by an announcer. Each brand had been given a three-letter name selected from a list of names that had been demonstrated to have no value connotations. The names used were Bix, Zim, Waz, and Biv. In the third scene the same person was shown with his personality significantly transformed in the direction predicted by the "drinking hypothesis."

After being shown these commercials, the subjects were allowed to taste the beers as much as they wanted, how they wanted, and to discuss them with each other. Each brand was contained in the same type of bottle with identical labels except for the name printed on them. Furthermore, and most important, was the fact unknown to the subjects: all four of the beers were exactly the same, from the same brew of the same brewery.

The subjects were not only asked to express their preferences, which they did with no difficulty, they were also asked to select one of the brands, a case of which would be given to them to take home. The percentage that chose the brand corresponding to their personality type was much larger than one would expect by chance. Furthermore, all the subjects believed the brands were different and that they could tell the difference between them. Most felt that at least one of the four brands was not fit for human consumption.*

These results not only confirmed the drinking hypothesis but also suggested an important direction for further research. A survey was designed and carried out in which beer drinkers were asked to characterize those whom they believed typically drank each major brand of beer marketed in their areas. This survey was carried out in six cities; 1200 subjects were interviewed. The results clearly revealed that each beer was perceived as having an appeal to particular personality clusters. Further research showed that those who drank each brand of beer

---

* These results showed that *in the short run only* drinkers could be induced to perceive differences that were not there. The experiment did not show that drinkers could be induced *not* to perceive differences that were there. Both Emery and we found distinctive taste preferences in each personality type. This meant that if a beer were to appeal to a particular type it had to have certain physical characteristics and not have others.

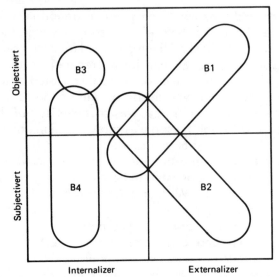

Figure 11.5. Personality segments associated with different brands of beer.

did in fact fall into these perceived clusters. The personalities associated with each brand not surprisingly corresponded to those of the people usually shown in their commercials. The personality segments found to be associated with four major brands of beer are shown in Figure 11.5.

Using this knowledge, it was possible to determine by further surveys what personality types drank each of the three brands A-B produces: Michelob, Budweiser, and Busch. Although these were found to have some overlap, in the main they were found to appeal to different personality segments of the market. This enabled us to determine which segments each brand was and was not reaching. From these surveys we were also able to estimate what portion of the beer consumed was consumed by each type. These portions varied significantly. Using this information, we were then able to specify target market segments to be reached either by existing brands or by new ones, *and now we knew what kind of advertising messages would be most effective in doing so.*

For example, although it was found that Michelob had most of its market in one part of the personality space, a small portion of its consumers were drawn from a different part of this space, a part in which the largest percentage of beer drinkers fell. This led to an advertising campaign directed at the second segment. The campaign succeeded in significantly increasing this brand's share of the target market.

The implications of these results to the preparation of advertising messages and the design of products is clear, but the typology and the theory based on it could be used in another less apparent way. We hypothesized different usage of different media by different personality types. For example, we predicted that reparative drinkers (objective internalizers) would watch more television than social drinkers (subjective externalizers), because reparatives are more likely to observe others and socials are more likely to be doing things, participating. The chances that a reparative will watch at least six hours of television on a non-work day, for example, are more than two and a half times greater than for a social. This ratio is even higher for indulgents, as one would expect. It is also possible to predict which magazine appeals to each type. For example, *Playboy* is almost twice as likely to be read by an oceanic as by an indulgent; the reverse is true for *Readers Digest*. Objective types (oceanics and reparatives) read newspapers more regularly and thoroughly than subjectives.

By combining information on the segmentation of the market with the information gained about the use of media, it became possible to combine messages and media in such a way as to direct advertising messages at particular market segments in a more effective way.

Our typology and personality theory has enabled A-B to gain insights into marketing phenomena that do not involve advertising. For example, research was undertaken for the company to determine what happens in a market when a new competitor enters it. In particular, the company was interested in identifying the personality characteristics of those who are most likely to try a new brand when it is introduced, those who switch to it as their regular brand, and the way others subsequently learn about the brand. Research was conducted in a number of markets that had experienced new brand entries in the relatively recent past. This work revealed that different personality types have significantly different likelihoods of trying new products. One of the types purchases new products thirty percent faster than the overall average. A second type does so slightly more than average, a third type slightly less, and the fourth type forty percent less than average. Furthermore, we found that those who are identified as early triers are influenced by advertising differently from those who switch to the product after it becomes established. The understanding thus gained enabled Anheuser-Busch to develop more effective advertising and other marketing strategies at appropriate times before, during, and after the introduction of new products.

Knowledge is power, and understanding is control; they are double-edged swords. To obtain knowledge and understanding of human behavior is to gain the ability to control the behavior of others more effectively either in one's own or their interests. Like any instrument, knowledge and understanding can be used for either good or evil—for example, an axe can be used to free a person from a burning building or to murder him. The use of every instrument necessarily involves ethical and moral judgments which cannot be avoided by the manager who uses the knowledge and understanding produced by research or by the researcher who produces them.

The understanding of drinking behavior developed in the research described here can be used to either intensify or ameliorate the "drinking problem." Fortunately, Anheuser-Busch believes it is in the long-run interests of the producers of alcoholic beverages as well as of their consumers to ameliorate it. One of the principal ways the company is using this understanding is in the development of more effective ways of preventing and treating alcoholism.

CHAPTER TWELVE

On Keeping Problems Solved

Few problems, once solved, stay that way. Changing conditions tend to *un*solve problems that previously have been solved.

A number of years ago a group of us at the University had worked long and hard to determine whether a major oil company should lease tankers or build its own. We studied the current and future availability of oil and leasable tankers, the costs of building, operating, and leasing tankers, and the future demand for oil. From this we concluded that, because of a virtually certain oversupply of leasable tankers, it would be less expensive to lease them than build new ones. The company accepted our recommendations and began their implementation.

A short while later the Egyptian-Israeli conflict broke out, and the Suez Canal was closed. This immediately created a world-wide shortage of tankers because they had to circumnavigate Africa when bringing oil from the Middle East to Europe or America, and this lengthened their trips considerably.

The closing of the Suez Canal was a conspicuous change of circumstances that made it immediately apparent to the company's decision makers that the solution they had accepted and started to implement was no longer a good one. It was changed quickly, adapting to the new set of environmental conditions.

The degradation of solutions is seldom as apparent or sudden as it was in this case, but it is common. Thus the wise problem solver constantly monitors solutions to past problems to be sure they are meeting his expectations. If they are not, he finds out why and modifies them.

The problems that manage to stay solved often create new problems. For example, one who has difficulty getting to work may solve this problem by purchasing an automobile, but the possession of a car creates all sorts of new problems such as obtaining insurance, maintenance, finding parking places, and so on. Therefore, the wise problem solver not only monitors previous solutions, but he also keeps alert and constantly scans his horizon to identify new problems that have arisen or will arise unless preventive action is taken.

Because problems do not stay solved and their solutions create new problems, a problem-solving system requires more than an ability to solve problems; it also requires the ability to maintain or control solutions that have been implemented and an ability to identify problems when or before they arise. In addition to these functions, a problem-solving system should be able to provide the information that the performance of these functions requires.

Problem solving requires a *system,* because the three primary functions—solving problems, controlling solutions, and identifying and anticipating problems—together with the supporting information function, are very interdependent. Therefore, the more effectively their interactions are designed and organized, the more effective problem solving can be.

The problem-solving system of large organizations may involve a number of different groups, each responsible for a different function or subfunction, but even in the case of an individual problem solver each of the functions should be present.

A great deal has been learned about how these functions can be organized and carried out. Here I try to provide a summary of this knowledge. First I consider the overall design of a problem-solving system, then I take up the individual functions that are necessary parts of it.

Figure 12.1 provides a diagrammatic representation of the system I describe. The numbers on the flows in the diagram and the letters in the boxes help tie the description and the diagram together.

As we have seen, every problem involves one or more controlled variables and one or more that are uncontrolled. The set of uncontrolled variables constitutes the relevant *environment* (A) and the set of controlled variables is the individual or system, effective manipulation of which is the objective of problem solving. I call this the *problem-object* (B) or simply *object*. The object of an individual's problem-solving efforts may, of course, be or include himself; for example, he may not feel well or be dissatisfied with his appearance.

To know that one has a problem or to know the nature of a problem that one has requires information about the problem-object and its environment. Therefore, *observation* of this object and its environment

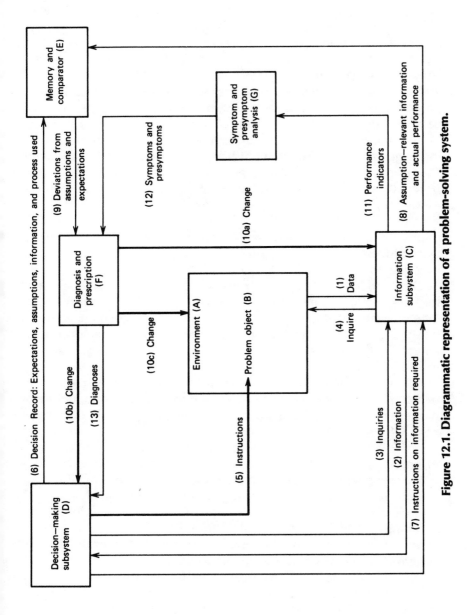

Figure 12.1. Diagrammatic representation of a problem-solving system.

is necessary. Observation is a process the output of which is *data* (1). Data consist of symbols that represent properties of object and events. They are raw material that require processing to convert them into *information* (2). Information also consists of symbols that represent the properties of objects and events, but these differ from those which are data in their *usefulness*. For example, a manager may ask his assistant to determine the dollar value of his company's finished-goods inventory. The assistant knows that finished goods are stored at three points. Therefore, he obtains a list of all items and determines the number stored at each point. Then he determines the selling price of each item. All this constitutes data. By addition and multiplication (i.e., *data processing*), he calculates the total value of the inventory. This constitutes information, because the manager can use it in his decision making. Data processing or information production is a major function of the *information subsystem* (C).

Data and information are relative concepts in the sense that symbols that are useful to one decision maker may not be useful to another. One manager may need to know the cubic feet of storage occupied by finished-goods inventory, another its dollar value. Data processing is an activity that was largely carried out by clerks in the past, but now is increasingly done by computers.

When a problem solver receives information—from himself, others, or a computer—he does not always find it useful. He may find it incomprehensible or unreadable, doubt its validity, or question its completeness. On the other hand, he may accept it but think of more information that he wants. For example, a large total value of a finished-goods inventory may lead him to want to know the value at each storage point separately, or which items are most responsible for the size of the inventory. For these or other reasons, the receipt of information often leads to *inquiries* (3) that require either additional information or "redoing" the information already received.

Inquiries require two additional capabilities in the information subsystem. The subsystem must be able to generate new data—that is, *inquire* (4) into the problem-object and its environment so that the necessary *data* (1) are obtained. It must also have the ability to reuse data that were previously received and, possibly, used. This means that it must be able to store data in such a way as to be able to retrieve them when necessary. A data-storage facility is, of course, a *file* whether in a drawer or a computer. A large computerized data-storage facility is often called a *data bank*.

Once the new or old data have been reprocessed to provide the information that constitutes a reply to the inquiry that initiated the process, it is transmitted to the *decision-making subsystem* (D). This inquiry-information cycle may continue until either the problem solver has all the information he wants or feels he has run out of time and must make a decision using whatever information he has, or that the cost and time of further inquiry is not likely to be justified by the additional or improved information it would yield.

To make a decision is to select a solution. This selection process has, of course, been discussed extensively in this book. However, I have a few more things to say about it in what follows. The output of a decision-making process is also a set of symbols, an *instruction* (5), that is transmitted to the problem-object which may be the instructor himself. An instruction is a communication to others or oneself that is intended to affect the behavior of the problem-object. For example, the solution to a weight problem may be an instruction to oneself to go on a diet. The problem solver or others who are part of the problem-object are expected to *implement* the solution.

Now let us consider what is required to monitor and control the solution once the relevant instruction has been issued. Every decision (solution) has one of two purposes: to make something happen that would not happen otherwise, or to prevent something from happening that otherwise would. In either case there is one or more expected effects and times by which these are expected. To control a solution, these expected effects and times of realization should be made explicit. Additionally, the assumptions on which these expectations are based and the information and decision-making process used in reaching them should also be made explicit. Together these make up the *decision-record* (6) which should be stored in an *inactive* memory (E). Human memories are generally much too active for this purpose. They have a way of restructuring the past that is counterproductive in this context for reasons that the next fable reveals.

Fable 12.1.   THE EXPECTATIONS THAT DROWNED IN A POOL.

The university-based research group of which I am a part was asked by a company with which we had worked in the past to develop a finished-parts inventory-control system. In a meeting with the company's executives in which the project was launched, I suggested that we have a little fun by setting up a pool on the project's outcome. Each executive would write on a piece of paper what effect on the size of the parts inventory he believed the study would have. This was to be expressed

Fable 12.1. The expectations that drowned in a pool. Moral: Contrary to what is commonly believed, memory can improve with age.

as a percentage increase or decrease. These expectation were to be written on a piece of paper that would be placed in an envelope, sealed, and signed on the outside. The envelopes were to be given to the corporate secretary for storage until the project was completed. Additionally, each executive was to put up $10, thus creating a pool that would go to the one whose expectations turned out to be closest to the eventual fact. The executives agreed and prepared their envelopes, and these were put away.

The study took about a year, during which there were frequent meetings between the researchers and executives. Each aspect of the work in progress was discussed thoroughly.

When the study was completed and the final report was about to be submitted, the executives were told that the envelopes had inadvertently been misplaced and could not be found, but that all was not lost. Each executive was given a fresh piece of paper and an envelope and asked to record what he had put down as his expectation a little more than a year earlier. They did so.

Once the envelopes were collected the "lost envelopes" were brought out, and the contents of the new and old ones were compared openly. The average of the earlier entries was about a fifty percent decrease in the parts inventory. The average of the "recalled expectations" was about a three hundred percent *increase* which was very close to the change brought about by the study.

> **MORAL: Contrary to what is commonly believed, memory can improve with age.**

Memory erases mistakes and thus prevents our learning from them. Since learning is an important objective of the solution-control subsystem, an inactive memory is required for the storage of decision-records.

The decision-record should be used to inform the information subsystem what information is needed to monitor the solution (7). The assumptions should be checked periodically to see if they still hold, and the actual effects of the solution (8) should be observed and brought together with the decision-record. The actual and assumed conditions and the actual and expected effects should be *compared* (E).

If nothing more than this were done, significant improvements in decision making are possible. This was dramatically shown in an experiment conducted in one of our major corporations by one of its management scientists. He had developed a set of equations that were able to reproduce accurately the past performance of his company given the executive decisions that had been made and the environmental conditions that had pertained. He then put these equations into a computer and set up the following experimental game.

Using managers in the company, he organized teams to act as the corporation's executive office. These teams were told that the objective of the game was to see how much better they could do than the corporation had actually done. Each team was required to make executive decisions for forty consecutive quarters. Once they did so for a particular quarter, their decisions were fed into the computer, and they received in return a profit-and-loss statement and a balance sheet. Their quarterly performances were plotted sequentially. Every team's performance improved over time, as expected.

Then a second set of an equal number of teams was set up. These teams had exactly the same assignment as the teams in the first set, but there was one procedural difference. Once a team in the second set had made its decisions, it was required to prepare a P&L statement and a balance sheet expressing the *expected effects* of its decisions. Its decisions were then fed into the computer which provided its output. These teams were then able to compare their explicitly formulated expectations with "actual performance."

The average rates of improvement of the first and second sets of teams were then compared. The second set learned significantly more rapidly than the first. This showed the value to decision makers of doing nothing more than explicitly formulating expectations and comparing them with actual performance. The problem-solving system being designed here, however, goes much further than this.

Where assumed and actual conditions, or expected and actual effects, agree, nothing need be done. All that needs to be noted are *deviations* (9) of actual from assumed conditions and actual from expected effects. Such deviations indicate that something has gone wrong. To determine what has and what should be done about it requires *diagnosis* (F).

The diagnostic function is to find the causes of deviations and to *prescribe* corrective action. Although the causes may be difficult to identify, they are only of four types.

1. *The information used in making the decision was in error,* and therefore the information subsystem requires *change* (10a) so that it will not repeat that type of error. For example, information about a competitor's production capacity may have been in error. If this is the case, a way should be sought to reduce the chances of such an error in the future as, for example, by obtaining information about competition from more reliable sources.

2. *The decision-making process may have been faulty,* for example, in failing to take into account important competitive reactions to a company initiative. In such a case a *change* in the decision-making procedure (10b) should be made, for example, by requiring the use of a counter-measure team in reaching any decision affecting competitors directly.

3. *The decision may have been correct, but it was not implemented as intended.* In such a case *changes* (10c) are required to

improve either communication of instructions or the organization or its personnel so that they are more likely to carry out instructions as intended in the future.

4. *The environment changed in a way that was not anticipated,* for example, the closing of the Suez Canal. In such cases a way of better anticipating such changes, decreasing sensitivity to them, or reducing their likelihood should be found. These may require any one or combination of the three types of change already mentioned or efforts to change the environment. For example, a law may be sought that would limit the fluctuation of raw material costs over specified periods of time, as is the case on the Commodity Exchange, or insurance may be obtained to protect against losses due to uncontrollable events.

The diagnostic and prescriptive function assures both *learning* (improving efficiency under constant conditions) and *adaptation* (maintaining or improving efficiency under changing conditions). That this is the case has been demonstrated in practice.

The marketing department of one large corporation set up a system of this type for monthly decisions that affected each of approximately two hundred marketing areas. The measure of performance used was market share in each area. A set of computerized models enabled the executives to explore the effects of different decisions before making them. The decisions covered the pricing of more than forty products, promotional activity, advertising levels, media mix, and timing, point-of-sales expenditures, and the company's field-selling effort. When a set of decisions was finally made for a marketing area, the computer generated the expected effect.

In the first month of operation this system identified forty-two deviants in the set of approximately two hundred decisions, and the average error of estimates of market share was about four percent. The diagnostic and prescriptive team went to work on these and was able to take action on most of them before the second month's decisions were made. The others were handled subsequently. The team was able to catch up with the work load, because the number of deviants was reduced in subsequent months. By the twelfth month there were only six deviants and in the eighteenth only two. The system then stabilized at about this level. In reaching this stability the average error of expectations was reduced to a fraction of one percent. Over this same period the company enjoyed a very large increase in its share of the national market.

Most of the deviants were easy to identify and correct—for example, the opening of a new chain of stores that used the company's products or the death of a wholesaler. Those which were more difficult to identify often required research to uncover and to prescribe for, for example, where per capita consumption increased and the reason for it had to be found.

In a decision-making system that can learn and adapt so effectively, little time and effort must go into trying to "optimize" initial decisions.

Now consider the *problem identification and anticipation subsystem* (G-F).

We normally use the term "symptom" to mean an indicator of a threat to the health of an organism or an organization. However, it may also be an indicator of an opportunity; that is, it may indicate that something is exceptionally good as well as exceptionally bad. A symptom is one of a range of values of a variable that usually occurs when something is exceptionally right or wrong but seldom when things are normal. Thus a fever is an abnormally high body temperature that is seldom associated with good health but is often associated with bad health. A high rate of inflation is usually taken to indicate that something is wrong with an economy, a low rate that something is right. An unusually small number of defects coming off a production line indicates that something is usually right, and there is an opportunity for the permanent improvement of its performance.

Variables used as symptoms are properties of behavior or performance of organisms or organizations. Such variables can also be used dynamically as *presymptoms* or *omens*: indicators of future opportunities or problems. For example, the range of normal body temperature is about one degree Farenheit. Suppose that in five consecutive readings of a person's temperature taken half an hour apart, normal but rising temperatures are observed. This would indicate that, unless there is an intervention, that person will have a fever in the near future. The same sort of thing would be true if we observed small but repeated increases in the number of defects coming off a production line.

A presymptom is *nonrandom normal behavior*. The nonrandomness may take the form of a trend or a cycle, among other things. There are many statistical tests for nonrandomness, but even the naked eye and common sense can identify most of them.

A complete problem-solving system regularly obtains *information on a number of performance indicators* (11) some of whose values are symptoms. In many organizations this is the function of the controller; in a hospital it is the function of nurses. Controllers and nurses usually obtain and examine a large number of performance indicators in search for symptoms and presymptoms. Therefore, in a complete problem-solving system the information subsystem (C) is responsible for obtain-

ing and providing measures of a number of characteristics of performance (11). It supplies them for *symptom and presymptom analysis* (G).
When symptoms or presymptoms are found, they become an input to
the diagnostic process (12). Once a diagnosis (13) is obtained, it is fed
into the decision-making process (D) where something is done about
it. A prescription or instruction (5) is issued.

Now we have all the necessary components and flows between
them for a complete problem-solving system. The entire system, of
course, may lie within a single individual, or it may lie within a large
organization in which mechanical means of observation, communication, and symbol manipulation are used extensively. Much of the
process can be automated. The extent to which the various functions
in the system can be automated varies, depending on the state of our
knowledge and our understanding of the functions.

The information subsystem can be automated to a large extent by
the use of computers. The selection of variables to use as symptoms
and their analysis can also be automated using techniques and procedures of statistical quality control. The memory and comparator can
also be virtually completely automated. Decision-making can be automated to some extent and diagnosis very little.

Because of developments in the decision sciences, some decisions
can be completely automated and others can be automated partially.
Recall that in principle every problematic situation can be represented
by a symbolic model of the form:

$$P = f(C_i, U_j)$$

in which

> $P =$ a measure of performance of the object, organism, or
> organization involved,
> $C_i =$ the controlled variables,
> $U_j =$ the uncontrolled variables, and
> $f =$ the relationship between the preceding variables.

Constraints that apply to any of the variables can usually be expressed
in symbolic form also.

Solving a problem consists of finding a set of values of the controlled variables that—under the environmental conditions defined by
the values of the uncontrolled variables and the relevant constraints—
produce a satisfactory level of performance. Models of some problem
situations are already available. In some others they can be tailor-made.

It is possible to specify a procedure of manipulating the symbols in some models to obtain a solution. Such a procedure is called an *algorithm*.

Where a symbolic model and an algorithm are available, problem solving can be completely automated. In general this can only be done in situations in which individual human choice does not play a major role. In industry such problems include production and inventory control, scheduling operations, the allocation of resources, and the location of facilities. Such problems tend to involve operations and tactics rather than strategy.

Then there is a set of more complex problems for which models but not algorithms are available. These can be used in a manager-machine dialogue. Although a model cannot be used to select a best solution without an algorithm, it can be used to evaluate any solution proposed to it. Thus it can be used to compare alternative solutions proposed by a manager. This makes possible a manager-machine dialogue that leads to a decision. The dialogue may be iterative, a sequence of steps that converge on a choice. For example, a manager proposes several solutions to a computer that contains the model. The computer compares them and feeds its evaluation back to the manager who uses it to formulate a new set of alternatives that he submits to the computer. This cycle can be continued until the manager obtains a solution he considers good enough or time has run out.

For example, a manager may have a computerized model that is capable of estimating the operating cost of a warehouse if its location is given. His problem may be to find a good location for it, say, anywhere in the United States. Initially he could select, for example, five widely dispersed locations and have these evaluated. The next set of alternatives he proposes can be clustered around the one that came out best in the first trial. This process can be continued until at least an approximately best location is identified.

Finally, there are those decisions which cannot be modeled and therefore must be made by decision makers using whatever internal and external resources are available to them. These are usually the most complex problems—ones that are strategic and normative rather than tactical and operational and involve human choice behavior in some significant way.

Managers once feared that the management sciences would eventually replace them with models, algorithms, and computers. This fear has diminished for two reasons. First, managers have come to realize that solving one problem usually creates one or more new ones, and these are often more difficult to solve than the original problem. Thus the effect of models, algorithms, and computers on managers is not to replace them but to require them to deal with more complex, strategic, and people-oriented problems. Unless managers develop the ability to deal with such problems, the management sciences can make them obsolete. These sciences reduce the need for specific managers, but not the need for management. Their principal effect is to raise the qualifications required to manage effectively.

Second, most managers have come to realize that most models do not cover all aspects of the problem situation to which they apply. They leave out critical variables that for one reason or another are not quantified at the present time. Thus the solutions obtained from most models tend to be partial and require a manager to add something. They provide an input to his decisions, not a substitute for them.

For example, models are available that can be used to locate a facility to minimize transportation costs of materials to or from that location. However, the qualitative characteristics of labor, their union, or the building sites available at these locations cannot be covered by models at the present time. Nevertheless such factors must be taken into account by managers. A solution yielded by such a model can be ridiculous because of its incompleteness. I can recall using a model of this type to find the so-called "best" location of a centralized parts warehouse in England. The "best" location acording to the model turned out to be in one of England's most expensive residential suburbs. Managers, using their knowledge of the relevant missing variables, were able to find a suitable location nearby.

It should also be kept in mind that even though a computer may solve a problem, responsibility for that solution is not the computer's or even its programmers'; it lies with the manager who is responsible for the function served by the solution.

A problem that can be modeled adequately and for which an algorithm exists can be said to be *understood*. Thus managers are not required where problems are *completely* understood—only management scientists are. However, few, very few, problems are completely understood and the skill required of a manager is precisely that of being able to find good solutions to problems where understanding is not complete. This does not mean that a manager performs best where he has least understanding. A simile helps make this clear. Think of a manager as a broadjumper trying to jump as far as he can into what is not yet understood. How far he can jump depends on his jumping ability and the height of the platform from which he jumps; the higher the platform, the further he can jump. The height of the platform corresponds to the amount of understanding he has or is provided to him by man-

Applications

agement scientists. It should be kept in mind that it is the manager, not the management scientist, who jumps and takes the associated risks.

So much for decision making (D); now consider the steps involved in control (E-F). First a decision record (6) must be produced. If the decision is made by men, they must prepare the record of their decision. This cannot be automated. If a computer made the decision, it can provide all the information required for the decision record except the assumptions on which the model it uses is based. These must be made explicit by those who develop the model. Too often this is not done. It is a responsibility of management to see that it is.

The storage of decision records and comparison of assumptions and expectations with what actually occurs can be completely automated. There are many good statistical procedures available for carrying out the comparison, and most of these have been programmed for use by computers.

The diagnosis of organizational and institutional problems can seldom be automated. Some progress has been made in automating the diagnosis of malfunctioning of machines and even of biological organisms. Further progress can be expected, but in the meantime scientists have something more than ordinary skills in finding causes of effects. Thus scientists, particularly management scientists, can often help in the diagnostic process.

Once the causes are identified, prescription is required. To prescribe is to decide what to do about a problem. Everything I have said about decision making in general applies to prescription in particular.

As noted above, symptom and presymptom analysis can be completely automated using the techniques of statistical quality control. However, the selection of variables to be screened for their ability to yield symptoms and presymptoms requires people who know a great deal about the system and what kinds of data it does and can generate.

Finally, there is the information subsystem. This aspect of problem-solving systems, particularly in the context of management, has been studied extensively. Information subsystems can be automated, but many, if not most, of these systems have failed to match the expectations of their users. I have tried to diagnose and prescribe for these deviants in another place (Ackoff, 1967). I want to mention only one aspect of this earlier work here. Most managers, if not decision makers in general, suffer less from lack of relevant information than from an overabundance of irrelevant information. This is not a play on words; it has significant consequences in the design of information systems.

It is common knowledge that most managers suffer from information overload; therefore, providing them with additional information, even relevant information, can help little because they do not have the time required to separate the wheat from the chaff. Increasing an overload has been shown to decrease the use of what information is available, because it heightens the frustration that is associated with the realization that only an insignificant portion of what is available can be absorbed.

For this reason an effective information system should *filter* information, eliminating the irrelevant, and *condense* what is relevant. There are few formal information systems that perform either of these functions. Yet they can be automated. A description of such a system designed to serve scientists and technologists can be found in Ackoff, Cowan et al. (1976).

Finally, it should be noted that a large number of skills other than those usually possessed by managers can contribute to effective decision making. These include the skills of management scientists, information-system specialists, statisticians, and behavioral and organizational scientists. It is becoming increasingly clear that in large complex organizations such skills should be fused into a management *system* that manages the organization. Managers increasingly do not manage the organization but manage the system that manages the organization.

The design and operation of an effective management system can benefit as much from creativity as can problem solving. However, this is another subject that would require another book for adequate treatment.

The task set for this book—how to solve problems more creatively— is now finished, or as finished as I can make it at this time. I hope the reader who has come with me up to this point feels that his effort and time were justified.

SOME SUGGESTED READINGS

My student and colleague Elsa Vergara has recently reviewed the extensive literature on *creativity*. Out of her reading she selected eight books that she considers to be the most useful to one interested in the subject. Here they are with her annotations.

Adams, James, *Conceptual Blockbusting*, San Francisco Book Co., San Francisco, 1976.
> Adams concentrates on what he calls "conceptual blocks" that are "mental walls which block the problem solver from correctly perceiving a problem or conceiving its solution." Throughout the book he provides a series of exercises and techniques designed to overcome these blocks:

de Bono, Edward, *Lateral Thinking,* Harper, New York, 1973.
> de Bono introduces the concept of lateral thinking that is concerned with breaking old patterns of thought and creating new ones. The book provides a series of exercises that help to develop one's potential for lateral thinking. It is a pleasant and interesting how-to-do-it book.

Gordon, William, *Synectics,* Harper and Row, New York, 1962.
> Gordon describes the technique used by the Synectic Research Group in Cambridge, Massachusetts and the experience in group problem solving in a number of organizations. This technique is usually applied to technical problems and is based on the utilization of metaphor. Emphasis is placed on problem definition.

Koestler, Arthur, *The Act of Creation*, Dell Publishing Co., New York, 1973.
> An excellent book, full of innovative and challenging ideas. Koestler succeeds in synthesizing the points of view of different disciplines. He introduces the concept of *bisociation* which he defines as "the perceiving of a situation or idea in two self-consistent but habitually incompatible frames of reference." Humor, art, and science serve as the context of his discussion. This book is full of enlightening examples. An extensive bibliography is included.

Osborn, Alex, *Your Creative Power*, Charles Scribner's Sons, New York, 1949.
> This book contains a discussion of *brainstorming,* a technique useful in group problem solving. It is based on a distinction between the production and evaluation of ideas. Osborn provides a checklist to help in generating new ideas. It contains questions that can be used when one is faced with a problem.

Parnes, Sidney J. and Harold F. Harding, *A Source Book for Creative Thinking*, Charles Scribner's Sons, New York, 1962. (See Taylor below.)

Seissge-Krenke, Inge, *Probleme und Ergebnisse der Kreativitaetsforshung*, Hans Huber, Bern, 1974.

   A comprehensive review of the literature on creativity. It provides an overview of the research and training methods relevant to the subject. It includes a description of an experiment on the effects of environmental factors on the creativity of children.

Taylor, Irving A., *Perspectives in Creativity*, Aldine, Chicago, 1975.

   This and the Parnes book provide a collection of articles by the best-known researchers on creativity. They provide a good way of obtaining an overview of the ideas that prevail in the field.

REFERENCES

Ackoff, Russell L., "Management Misinformation Systems," *Management Science, 14* (1967), B-147–B-156.

——, *Redesigning the Future,* John Wiley & Sons, New York, 1974.

——, "Towards Flexible Organizations: A Multidimensional Design," *OMEGA, 5* (1977), 649–662.

——, T. A. Cowan, P. Davis, M. Elton, J. C. Emery, M. Meditz, and W. Sachs, *Designing a National Scientific and Technological Communication System: The SCATT Report,* University of Pennsylvania Press, Philadelphia, 1976.

——, and J. R. Emshoff, "Advertising Research at Anheuser-Busch, Inc. (1963–68)," *Sloan Management Review, 16* (Winter 1975), 1–15.

——, "Advertising Research at Anheuser-Busch, Inc. (1968–74)," *Sloan Management Review, 16* (Spring 1975), 1–16.

Allport, G. W., and H. S. Odbert, "Trait-Names: A Psycholexical Study," *Psychological Monographs,* No. 211, 1936.

Bottiny, Walter, "Trends in Automobile Ownership and Indicators of Saturation," *Highway Research Record, 106* (1966).

Bureau of Public Roads, *Highway Statistics, Summary to 1965,* Washington, D.C., 1967.

Cars for Cities, Report of the Steering Group and Working Group Appointed by the Ministry of Transport, Her Majesty's Stationery Office, London, 1967.

Davis, Stanley M., and Paul R. Lawrence, *Matrix,* Addison-Wesley Publishing Co., Reading, Mass., 1977.

de Bono, Edward, *New Think,* Basic Books, New York, 1967.

Department of Housing and Urban Development, *Studies in New Systems of Evolutionary Urban Transportation,* Vol. II, Washington, D.C., 1968(a).

——, *Tomorrow's Transportation: New Systems for the Urban Future,* Washington, D.C., 1968(b).

Goggin, William C., "How the Multidimensional Structure Works at Dow Corning," *Harvard Business Review, 52* (January–February 1974), 54–65.

Hall, John R., Jr., and R. L. Ackoff, "A Systems Approach to the Problems of Solid Waste and Litter," *Journal of Environmental Systems, 2* (December 1972), 351–364.

Henry, Jules, *Culture against Man,* Random House, New York, 1963.

Laing, R. D., *The Politics of Experience,* Ballantine Books, New York, 1967.

208   References

Landsberg, Hans, L. Fleishman, and J. Fisher, *Resources in America's Future,* The Johns Hopkins Press, Baltimore, 1963.

Lansing, J. B., and G. Hendricks, *Automobile Ownership and Residential Density,* Survey Research Center, University of Michigan, Ann Arbor, 1967.

Lyle, C. Fitch and Associates, *Urban Transportation and Public Policy,* Chandler Publishing Co., San Francisco, 1964.

Management and Behavioral Science Center, *Planning and Design for Juvenile Justice,* U.S. Department of Justice, Law Enforcement Assistance Administration, Washington, D.C., August 1972.

McClenehan, J. W., and H. J. Simkowitz, "The Effect of Short Cars on Flow and Speed in Downtown Traffic: A Simulation Model and Some Results," *Transportation Science, 3* (1969), 126–139.

Minicar Transit System, Final Report of Phase I, Feasibility Study, prepared by the University of Pennsylvania for the U.S. Department of Transportation, 1968.

National Academy of Sciences, *U.S. Transportation Resources, Performance and Problems,* Proceedings of the Transportation Research Conference, Woods Hole, Mass., 1960.

Penn-Jersey Transportation Study, Vol. I: "The State of the Region," Philadelphia, 1964.

Rapoport, Anatol, *Fights, Games, and Debates,* The University of Michigan Press, Ann Arbor, 1960.

Roles et Fonctions Futurs de Paris: Ville Internationale, Documentation du Gouvernement Francais, Paris, Publication No. 39, 1973.

Sagasti, Francisco, and R. L. Ackoff, "Possible and Likely Futures of Urban Transportation," *Socio-Economic Planning Science, 5* (1971), 413–428.

Schon, Donald, *Beyond the Stable State,* Random House, New York, 1971.

Singer, E. A., Jr., *In Search of a Way of Life,* Columbia University Press, New York, 1948.

Toffler, Alvin, *Future Shock,* Bantam Books, New York, 1971.

Waid, Clark, D. F. Clark, and R. L. Ackoff, "Allocation of Sales Effort in the Lamp Division of the General Electric Company," *Operations Research 4* (1956), 629–647.

Wilbur Smith and Associates, *Transportation and Parking for Tomorrow's Cities,* New Haven, 1966.

Index